Stephen Kew

Handicap and Family Crisis

A study of the siblings of handicapped children

Pitman Publishing

First published 1975

Pitman Publishing Ltd
Pitman House, 39 Parker Street, London WC2B 5PB, UK

Pitman Medical Publishing Co. Ltd
42 Camden Road, Tunbridge Wells, Kent TN1 2QD, UK

Focal Press Ltd
31 Fitzroy Square, London W1P 6BH, UK

Pitman Publishing Corporation
6 East 43 Street, New York, NY 10017, USA

Fearon Publishers Inc
6 Davis Drive, Belmont, California 94002, USA

Pitman Publishing Pty Ltd
Pitman House, 158 Bouverie Street, Carlton, Victoria 3053,
Australia

Pitman Publishing
Copp Clark Publishing
517 Wellington Street West, Toronto M5V 1G1, Canada

Sir Isaac Pitman and Sons Ltd
Banda Street, PO Box 46038, Nairobi, Kenya

Pitman Publishing Co. SA (Pty) Ltd
Craighall Mews, Jan Smuts Avenue, Craighall Park,
Johannesburg 2001, South Africa

© Invalid Children's Aid Association 1975

ISBN 0 273 00801 3

Reproduced and printed by photolithography and bound in
Great Britain at The Pitman Press, Bath
G4594 : 11

Preface

The ideas and illustrations presented in this book represent what
is in many ways a personal and subjective view of handicap. In
the course of my work with the Invalid Children's Aid Association,
I have assessed and evaluated evidence of various sorts concerning the problems facing families with a handicapped child. In
writing about these problems here I have tried as far as possible
to present them in a well-illustrated and documented way which
will be of use or interest (but hopefully both) to social workers,
laymen and all those families who themselves have a handicapped
child. It should be appreciated, however, that although I have
been systematic in the way I have collected information, and
although I have tried to be fair in presenting it, this is not a
report on a strictly controlled study, nor are its conclusions
'scientifically' reached. It may well be that more thorough
research will place the emphasis in a different way on the various
problems I have outlined, or that it will discard altogether some
of the assumptions and inferences I have made.

I have given an account in chapter 2 of the particular methods
I adopted in making this study. I feel, however, that there are a
number of points in relation to my approach which ought to be
made right away.

Quite a lot of discussion has taken place recently, particularly amongst academics who approach disability from the point
of view of comparative research, (e.g. Sheila Hewett, Ann Gath),
as to whether or not the family of the handicapped child, and in
some cases the siblings of the handicapped child, are measurably
different from 'ordinary' families and siblings. It should be
understood that this book is not a contribution to that particular
debate, nor does it incorporate comparative data relating to it.
This means of course that when I talk, for example about the
jealousy of certain siblings towards their handicapped brothers

Handicap and Family Crisis

and sisters, I may well be talking about a phenomenon which occurs amongst a similar proportion of so-called 'ordinary' siblings. Obviously we would ideally want to know whether or not this was the case, and it is a deficiency of any study based on essentially subjective assessment and analysis that it cannot give an answer to such questions.

To base a book primarily on case material lays one open to a number of legitimate criticisms on other grounds as well. In relying heavily on the experience of social workers, for example many biases and prejudices, both my own and those of the social workers concerned, will inevitably have been incorporated into the points of view expressed, and may well underlie the selection of the particular areas I have chosen to explore. Furthermore, in using caseworkers' descriptions of what is happening in particular families, it may legitimately be argued that I have achieved only a second-hand view of the problems facing the siblings and parents concerned.

There are many sound reasons for the current trend of letting the client speak for himself. Of course, against this it can be claimed that parents and siblings are the last to understand what is happening in their own family group, and that only someone who is close to them and their problems, yet who remains emotionally detached from the problem itself, is in a position to see what is going on in the family as a whole. Also, of course, there are many points in favour of using information collected by social workers on home visits over a period of months in preference to the information collected by researcher who appear on the doorstep one morning with a list of obligatory questions. Be that as it may, it would be pointless to deny that these weaknesses exist, and one should clearly be aware of them when basing judgements on the material that I have presented.

My excuse for continuing with the book despite all these shortcomings is that a problem undoubtedly exists about which little has previously been written. A wealth of relevant material was available to me, and however problematic that material may be it seemed a pity not to use it, if only as a stop-gap until a more worthwhile study could be made.

I am deeply indebted to the ICAA for allowing me the time and resources to write this book, and to all of the staff at the Keith Grove Centre who so patiently put up with me while I wrote it. I would particularly like to thank Eileen Roome and Jill Vincent who gave me much needed help and encouragement, also

iv

Preface

he caseworkers from the London offices who complied so
·eadily with my various requests for help, and the many typists
vho so patiently and accurately deciphered my writing. Dr
ᵖhilip Graham from Great Ormond Street Hospital kindly agreed
ᵒ read the manuscript and made many useful suggestions.

Finally I would like to express my appreciation to the siblings
hemselves and to the other members of their families, who
shared their experiences in the first place with the other case-
vorkers and myself. Needless to say, their names and other
letails which might identify them have all been changed, though
he problems they live with have as far as possible been faithfully
·ecorded. If I have thrown just a little light on those problems,
hen the effort involved will have been well worthwhile.

S.K.

Contents

1 The problem

'Retardation is not primarily a problem that resides in an
individual, but rather is an event that occurs in a family and
a community.'

S. Sarason.

Social attitudes to handicap have undergone a quiet revolution in
recent years. More public money is being spent today than ever
before in an attempt to integrate the handicapped into the everyday
life of the community, more resources are being devoted to meeting their medical, social, and education needs, and a vast array
of different professions have addressed themselves in one way or
another to the problems raised by the birth and growth of the
handicapped child.

These developments in social awareness and action are long
overdue, but it is still sadly true that despite all the growing
interest and concern, many of the problems posed by handicap
have not yet been properly identified, yet alone met.

One reason for this is that professional concern has for a
very long time been monopolized by a concentric approach to
handicap. It has been concentrated, in other words, on the handicapped child himself - on his feelings, his problems, his needs -
and in doing so it has largely failed to see handicap as a social
event in the context of the family and the community in which it
occurs.

It is, of course, true that the problems of education,
rehabilitation, transport, medical treatment, home care and
employment, to name but a few, which face the severely handicapped child, are extremely real and pressing problems. Without a doubt they deserve all the attention they receive from the
various specialized professional bodies whose task it is to tackle
them. But the fact remains that while the handicapped child
himself lies at the centre of professional concern, the needs of

1

the family and the community with respect to the handicapped child will continue to be largely unrecognized and unmet.

What I have tried to do in this book is to redress this balance by taking a different perspective on handicap. I have focused not on the disabled child himself but on his able-bodied brothers and sisters. From this approach it quickly emerged that many siblings face enormous social and emotional problems in relation to handicap, even though they themselves are healthy and sound of limb. Some of their problems arise directly out of their relationship with their handicapped brother or sister; most however, are related to changes which are wrought in the family as a whole as it tries to cope with and adjust to the birth and presence of a handicapped child.

In attempting to identify and describe the sibling's problems therefore, one is concerned with the whole nexus of relationships within the family. This being so, one is inevitably led into many areas of family functioning which may not, from a traditional point of view, appear to be valid subjects of concern for someone purporting to deal with the problems of physical and mental disability.

The fact is, however, as I hope to illustrate in the chapters which follow, that the family meaning of handicap goes very deep indeed. The birth of a handicapped child can, without any shadow of doubt, have a far-reaching effect upon every conceivable area of personal and family life, and although I have largely concentrated in this study on describing the difficulties faced by siblings I hope that I have at least cast some light on the other major problems which are likely to arise in other areas of the family. Economic hardship, marital crisis and parental feelings of guilt and anxiety, for example, quite apart from their potential effect on siblings, are worthy of a great deal more attention than they have so far received.

THE TWO APPROACHES TO HANDICAP

Before looking in more detail at the implications of a family-centred approach, it would be wise to take a closer look at the traditional or concentric approach to handicap so that we can distinguish more clearly between the problems that are already being tackled by the professional support systems in this field, and those which are inadvertently being neglected.

I have called a concentric approach one in which the special

needs of the handicapped child lie at the centre of our field of
vision and therefore at the centre of the social nexus we perceive.
The primary concern of social workers and others who take such
an approach is to identify the special needs of these children and
of the adults who care for them, and then to meet these needs.

It is not hard to see why researchers, writers and welfare
organizations alike have confined themselves to this sort of
approach for so many years, for the attention of each professional
group is automatically directed first and foremost to the handicapped child by the very nature of their professional roles.

Paediatricians and medical social workers, for example, have
traditionally worked strictly within the confines of the hospital.
The ward provides the setting for their work, therefore the needs
and feelings of the handicapped child himself have been their main
concern, though they have naturally paid due regard to the feelings
of parents on hospital visits and made some attempts to educate
them about the medical, emotional and educational needs of their
rather special children.

Researchers, for their part, are always attracted to the
externally different, so it is not surprising that they too have
concentrated on the handicapped child, his adjustment and his
experience of living with a stigma, rather than on his more
'normal' counterpart, the sibling.

Welfare agencies, on the other hand, who have perhaps had
the best chance to see handicap in a different perspective, have
very often been blinded by the immensity of the care-problems
facing parents with a severely disabled child. They have therefore tended to stop short at the provision of aids, holidays and
financial help to families in need. A number of things have
served to reinforce this role. For a start, many families refer
themselves initially with requests for practical help in coping
with their handicapped child even though underlying these requests
there are often quite different, though less easily verbalized
needs. Secondly, although the social worker may visit the parents
at home, these visits often occur when the father is at work and
the siblings at school so that the full extent of the problems
facing the family in the home is not seen.

All of these factors have conspired to establish the concentric
view of handicap as the mainstream approach. It is true, in fact,
that as a result of this approach great steps have been made in
coping with, catering for, and understanding the needs of handicapped children. What is not always realized, however, is that

3

these steps have often been accompanied by a distortion of vision
a professional myopia which has tended to ignore the other side
of the problem posed by a severely handicapped child for his
family.

It is only by taking the second, quite different view of handicap, that these problems begin to emerge. Instead of starting
with the handicapped child and tracing the needs and problems
which emanate from him, this second approach begins with the
family as a group, a group whose existence precedes the arrival
of the handicapped child. Handicap is thus seen not as the
affliction of one individual giving rise to a host of special needs,
but rather as a special sort of episode or event in the life of an
ordinary family group.

When we take this second perspective, the disabled child is
no more the centre of our interest than any other member of the
family. His needs, special though they may be, are balanced
against the needs of others and may often be found to be in
opposition to them. The important point about taking this family-
centred approach is that we are not blinded to the overall dynamic
of handicap by the special needs of one individual. In fact everyone's needs in this situation are special, and when we realize
this, we begin to see handicap in an altogether wider perspective
That is, as a social event which is capable of disrupting the
balance of forces in an entire family group.

There is certainly nothing new about the idea of a family-
centred approach; it has been applied with considerable success
in other fields of social work and psychiatry. For some reason,
however, it has rarely been applied in the field of handicap.
This means that many of the problems I shall be looking at in
the course of this book have not been properly examined elsewhere. The writer who takes a concentric view of handicap, with
the disabled child at the centre of his field of vision, will automatically tend to lose sight of the changes that are wrought in
such things as the marital relationship, the social relations of
the family within the community and, of more direct concern to
us here, the lives of the able-bodied siblings. That these areas
do not, in fact, receive the attention they deserve, is demonstrated by the bias in the existing provision of services in this
field. There is, for example, a statutory health-visiting service
to help parents with care problems relating to their handicapped
child, but if they receive help with, say, emotional or marital
problems arising from the impact of handicap, it will largely be

4

a matter of luck. The social service departments have a
statutory responsibility to help families with physical adaptations
and aids for the handicapped child, but there is no systematic
process of referring such families for other sorts of help, for
example with the enormous social readjustments they need to
make as a family.

These gaps in the existing services are in no way the fault
of individual social workers. They are clearly there as a result
of social policy, for the fact is that at present the 'official' view
of handicap is a concentric one, focusing primarily on the needs
of the handicapped child himself.

The consequences of a concentric approach

There are several important consequences of this bias in official
perspective. The first is that marital and sibling problems
which come to the attention of an agency or authority, often do so
only after a considerable period of time when a great deal of
damage has already been done. Help of the right sort at the right
time (i.e. before things have been allowed to deteriorate) could
undoubtedly have a preventive effect. Much has been written
about the need for prevention in the field of social casework but
there can be few instances where the potential cause of disturbance is so readily identifiable by an outside observer, and where
the population at risk is so easily accessible to help, as it is
with handicap.

The second consequence is that the sort of problems I have
been talking about may persist for a very long time even after
they have been 'picked up' by an agency, without anyone making
the vital connection between the problem (in whatever way it is
being expressed) and the presence of the handicapped child in the
family. In short, the connection between events is simply not
made because the events themselves are not perceived as a whole.
This is particularly true when help, advice or 'treatment' is
offered in an agency setting rather than in the home. In one
case that was reported to me, it was claimed that a sibling with
severe enuresis and symptoms of anxiety had been attending a
child guidance clinic for nearly a year before it was discovered
that he had a severely handicapped sister with whom his father
and mother were completely preoccupied. Obviously, it is hard
to establish the truth of such 'information', but it is true nevertheless that one visit to the family at home could immediately

have established the connection between handicap and the child's 'symptoms' and would have enabled the real nature of 'the probl to be seen more easily and quickly.

The third consequence of taking a concentric approach to handicap, and of the subsequent failure to see family problems i their true perspective, is somewhat different from the previous two. The consequences I have looked at so far have involved a failure either in perception or in action by the formal support systems within the community. But when the casework agencies hospitals, etc., view a handicapped child as the focus of all a family's problems and needs, the family themselves are implicitly encouraged to do the same. One thing I shall repeated stress in the chapters that follow is that handicap is a variable which cuts across an already existing situation - a situation, moreover, which is often highly complex and which may compris problems of every imaginable sort. When a social worker appears on the scene, therefore, and focuses attention on the handicapped child, many families will find a welcome excuse to project all their respective problems on to handicap, whereas ir reality handicap may well have been no more than the trigger which has brought problems to the surface whose real origin lay in other, quite unrelated directions. In such cases the professionals may well collude in the family's projection, without ever realizing what they are doing, simply because they are not looki at the family as a dynamic whole.

As I have already suggested, the final and most important consequence of relying exclusively on a concentric approach is that a whole range of family problems is in danger of being ignored. There is a growing amount of evidence which points to major upheavals and crises in numerous areas of family life. In a later chapter I will spend some time developing the concept of crisis in families with a handicapped child; at present it is enough to point out that the birth of a handicapped child is a potential source of disruption in the life of a family group, giving rise to needs which are often far removed from those of the chil himself.

Bernard Farber, for example, has shown that the relationship between a husband and wife who have a severely retarded child is likely to be poorer on average than the marital relationship for other couples. In a carefully constructed piece of research using questions relating to sexual relationships, verbal communication and many other relevant items, he was able to

devise a marital integration score for any married couple. He
then compared groups of parents who had a severely retarded
child with groups who were similar in all other respects but had
only able-bodied children. He found quite conclusively that the
parents in the former group, using the criteria he had selected,
attained on average a significantly lower marital integration
score than parents in the second group. This sort of result has
been confirmed by other researchers.

A second piece of evidence indicates that it is not only the
marital relationship that is likely to be disrupted in these
families. H.F.R. Prechtl conducted a research project on the
mother-child relationship when the babies in question had minimal
brain damage. The results from this fascinating study are all
the more important as none of the mothers was aware at the time
that their baby was in any way defective. Prechtl conducted his
research on a very large sample of mothers in a maternity
hospital before their babies had been diagnosed as brain damaged.
In this way he was able to obtain many closely matched controls
(i.e. mothers whose babies turned out to be quite normal). He
then used these controls comparatively to study the effect on the
relationship between mother and child when the baby in question
was abnormal, but not sufficiently so to have yet been diagnosed.

What he found, in fact, was that after a few months mothers
did not show a harmonious positive attitude to their baby in seven
out of eight of those cases where the baby eventually turned out
to be brain damaged. He pointed out that:

'in the first place they did not think that the source of the
problem was the baby itself but rather that they were 'mis-
handling' their child. In the second place the baby's behaviour
failed to satisfy the mother's expectations'.

These study-group mothers showed a higher approval of activity
by the child, fostered a greater dependency in him and were
generally less rejecting of their own home-making role than
mothers whose babies were not brain-damaged. Prechtl concludes that:

'These findings give evidence of the fact that the mothers of
abnormal babies, although they are not aware of it consciously,
are more protective and dominant.'

These two pieces of evidence taken together suggest that, quite
apart from any special needs which may be imposed by handicap,

there are important changes in the actual structure and quality of relationships in families where there is a handicapped child.

Farber's evidence shows that the relationship between husband and wife is likely to deteriorate in families with a retarded child, and from Prechtl's work we learn that the nature of the relationship between mother and child is likely to undergo an unconscious but unmistakable qualitative change when the child in question is minimally brain damaged. There is a great deal of other evidence to suggest that changes such as this are likely to take place whatever the handicap of the child and also in other sorts of relationships both inside and outside the family. I shall present this evidence in later chapters and also examine the effect on other relationships in more detail.

Although my main interest is in siblings, none of these potential problem-areas in family functioning can safely be ignored, for in taking a family-centred approach we inevitably find that changes in the dynamics of one relationship within the family will affect the dynamics of other relationships too.

Focusing on siblings

Having said that the family-centred approach has rarely been applied to the field of handicap, it is worth pointing out that a number of writers have paid homage to this sort of approach without ever really coming to terms with its full implications. Families, after all, are made up of children as well as parents, yet the able-bodied children in these families are quite often ignored by people purporting to look at the whole family group.

Thomas Jordan, for example, in 'The Mentally Retarded', (Merrill Books 1961), begins in this way:

'Mental retardation as a public issue - as a school problem, a medical problem or a rehabilitation problem - is of secondary significance. Attention to these matters is obviously important but it is justified only after we have seen the real proportion of the problem which is the significance of mental retardation as a family issue.'

He then devotes 45 pages to an outline of 'the family issue' but in all of this finds room only for three sentences on siblings. He is by no means alone in this extraordinary omission. The apparently exhaustive report of the National Bureau for Co-operation in Child Care, 'Living with Handicap', 1970, is a prime example of a concentric approach. Although stating in no uncertain terms the potentially disastrous effect that a handicapped child can have on a family, the authors' only definite comment on siblings in 370 pages is contained in the following sentence:

'As the parents' letters in connection with our enquiry vividly illustrate, the handicapped child's disability affects the lives of his parents and his brothers and sisters, both by presenting them with practical problems and by affecting their feelings about themselves and their relationships with others.'

But no other mention is made of the siblings or of the way in which their lives are affected. The writers of such reports, one feels, cannot really have looked at the family as a whole group, otherwise they would surely have taken some account of the children in the families they are describing.

The literature in this field is full of oblique and incidental references to the detrimental effect of handicap on siblings such as the ones I have just cited, but only rarely have these problems been looked at in their own right or in any real depth. On the whole they have simply been ignored. Perhaps this is because siblings are the members of the family who are most removed from problems of care and from the making of decisions in relation to the handicapped child. They lie somewhere on the outer circles of the visual field of those who take a concentric approach; they therefore become peripheral objects of concern.

Evidence of sibling disturbance

Despite this state of affairs there is a growing body of evidence to support the view that the sibling has a far worse time, pushed as he is into the background both of family affairs and of professional concern, than any other member of the family. At least one psychiatrist, Elva Poznanski, claims that

'Child psychiatrists see more siblings of the handicapped than handicapped children themselves'.

In a short but perceptive article, Poznanski confirms the view that sibling problems are often neglected by everyone around them.

'The handicapped child, in our culture, is the focus of much attention and the community increasingly provides specialized services for him. In his home the extra time and attention the child requires may burden the family, particularly his mother, such that it interferes profoundly with normal family activities. The underlying effects which this emphasis may have upon brothers and sisters often are unrecognized or neglected, both by the parents and the family paediatrician.'

What effect does this have on siblings? What are the problems they face? According to Poznanski the sibling's problems stem largely from changes in the relationship between mother and child. She says:

'The relationships of the mother with her other children often become distorted, at times severely, because of the extra time and attention the handicapped child requires. Understandably the other children tend to interpret this as meaning that they are less favoured and loved. For parents who have other problems, such as marital disharmony or personality difficulties, or lack of sensitivity to their children's emotional needs, the simple presence of the handicapped child may incite or aggravate unhealthy relationships among family members.'

Other writers have pointed to other sources of problems for siblings. In America, Meyer Schreiber and Mary Feeley ran a group exclusively for teenage siblings of the handicapped, and in England R.F. Coleman did the same. Both projects came to the same conclusion: that these children harboured many fears and anxieties relating to handicap - a conclusion that was endorsed by Michael Begab in 'The Mentally Retarded Child'. In 1967 Margaret Adams grew aware of the problems facing siblings and drew attention to them in an article in 'Child Welfare'. She distinguished between two sorts of problems: those that are common to most children in most family settings throughout the total childhood period and those of a more specific nature, which impinge crucially at difficult phases of development. She also maintained that there are two major areas of common difficulties the pervasive sorrow and anxiety which most parents experience on behalf of their handicapped child and which is a constant background feature in the environment of the sibling, and the danger of the normal child patterning his behaviour by identifying with the handicapped child in his early stages of development.

All of these people came across sibling problems on an individual level in their dealings with particular children or groups of children. Tizard and Grad, in 1961, and Joan McMichael, in 1971, both conducted surveys of a more general

statistical kind on families with handicapped children. Both
included questions on siblings and both came to similar conclusions: that some siblings have problems clearly related to
the impact of handicap on their family and that quite a large
number of siblings are emotionally disturbed. McMichael
divided her sample into four categories: (1) normal; (2) those
who showed a slight degree of failure to adjust; (3) those who
showed a moderately severe degree of failure to adjust and
(4) those who showed a severe degree of failure to adjust. She
found that 21 per cent of the siblings in her sample fell into the
latter two categories, a percentage similar to the one derived
by Tizard and Grad. It is interesting to compare this figure of
21 per cent with the findings reported by Kellmer Pringle in the
National Child Development Study. Here it was found that only
eight per cent of the country's total population of seven-year-old
children showed signs of emotional disturbance. Although the
sibling group would seem to show a significantly higher incidence
of disturbance, it should be remembered that different criteria
were used for rating disturbance in these respective surveys and
they are therefore not strictly comparable. However, all of
these pieces of evidence, taken together, do suggest that siblings
of the handicapped are very much a group at risk.

THE TASK

Here then we have a problem: it is a problem not only for the
individual members of a family but also for all those professionals
who have an interest, however oblique, in the field of handicap.
The particular task I have set myself here is to define the nature
of the risk to which siblings of the handicapped are exposed. I
have not set out to define this risk in quantitative terms by comparing samples of study siblings with matched samples of other
children. Worthy though such a task would have been, and
necessary though it is, it would have involved too many problems
in sampling and in the meaningful assessment of disturbance for
a small-scale study such as my own. What is perhaps more
important, it would have failed to use the most valuable resource
I have had at my disposal as an employee of the Invalid Children's
Aid Association - namely, a vast body of detailed and illuminating
case material from many hundreds of families, collected in depth
over years of intensive home visiting by family caseworkers.
    I have tried to put this material to good use by building up

from actual case studies a detailed picture of the major difficulties that siblings face. In doing this I hope it will become
clear that it is no longer enough to regard handicap simply as a
tragedy for the individual child, nor is it enough to direct our
resources towards meeting the specialized needs of the individual
alone. Handicap is a family event affecting the whole family
unit, and it is only by treating it as such that we will see the
problems it poses in their true perspective.

References

Adams, M. Siblings of the retarded - their problems and treat-
    ment. 'Child Welfare', XLVI, no. 6, 1967.

Begab, M. 'The Mentally Retarded Child - a Guide to Services of
    Social Agencies', Children's Bureau publications, no.404, 1963

Coleman, R.F. 'Groupwork with brain injured children and
    their siblings'. Report of the 4th Annual Conference of the
    Association for Children with Learning Disabilities. New
    York, 1967.

Farber, B. 'Effects of a Severely Retarded Child on Family
    Integration'. Monograph of Society for Research into Child
    Development, vol. 24 no. 2. Child Development Publications,
    1959.

Farber, B. 'Family Organization and Crises: maintenance of
    integration in families with a severely mentally retarded
    child'. Monograph of Society for Research into Child
    Development. 25 (whole no. 75) 1960.

Jordan, T. 'The Mentally Retarded'. Merrill Books, Ohio,
    1961.

Kellmer Pringle, M. Policy implications of child development
    studies. 'Concern', no. 3, November 1969.

McMichael, J. 'Handicap - a Study of Physically Handicapped
    Children and their Families'. Staples Press, London, 1971.

National Bureau for Co-operation in Child Care. 'Living with
    Handicap'. London, 1970.

Poznanski, E. Psychiatric difficulties in siblings of handicapped
    children. 'Clinical Paediatrics', vol. 8 no. 4, 1969.

Prechtl, H.F.R. The mother-child interaction in babies with
minimal brain damage. In 'Determinants of Infant Behaviour'
Vol. II, Ed. Brian Foss. Methuen, London, 1963.

Sarason, S. and Doris, J. 'Psychological Problems in Mental
Deficiency'. Harper & Row, New York, 1969.

Schreiber, M. and Feeley, M. Siblings of the retarded - a
guided group experience. In 'Management of the Family of
the Mentally Retarded', W. Wolfensberger and R.A. Kurtz
(Eds). Follett Educational Corporation, USA, 1969.

Tizard, J. and Grad, J.C. 'The Mentally Handicapped and
Their Families'. Oxford University Press, 1961.

2 Outline of approach

My primary aim in writing this book has been to draw upon the
experience of caseworkers at the ICAA and to use case material
compiled by them in order to describe and discuss the main
sorts of 'disturbance' affecting the siblings of handicapped children. I have tried at all times to view these disturbances and
difficulties in terms of a real family situation rather than as
isolated problems for the individuals concerned.

The study was entirely sponsored by the Invalid Children's
Aid Association. ICAA is a voluntary social work agency operating in and around London, which is different in at least two
respects from most other agencies working in the field of handicap. In the first place its interest in handicap is general, and
therefore handicaps of every variety, both physical and mental,
and every degree of severity are dealt with. This is in marked
contrast to the many organizations designed to promote the
interests of one particular group of handicapped people. The
second difference is that, unlike most organizations and social
service departments, its main concern is with the emotional
impact of handicap on the family.

Caseworkers visiting families at home have repeatedly
found that certain siblings are adversely affected by the birth,
presence and in some cases the institutionalization or death of a
handicapped child. Moreover they have found that their problems
quite commonly tend to be eclipsed by the more conspicuous
problems of the handicapped child himself.

The ICAA has regular casework contact with many hundreds
of families coming from every variety of social and economic
background. The wealth of information and experience they
possess in relation to the problems with which I am concerned,
is without question unique in this country. It is therefore an
ideal agency on which to base a study such as this.

I have had 'at my disposal' case material from the entire

· Outline of approach

range of families being visited by an ICAA worker and considered
relevant to the terms of this study - that is, families in which
there was at least one sibling and one handicapped child. (For
full details of omissions from this 'sample', see Appendix A.)
This amounted to a total of 538 families.

Using case material from this number of families poses
certain special problems in the collation of information and the
wide choice of material from which to select illustrations can be
a drawback as well as an advantage in so far as it increases the
subjective element of choice. However, I eventually set about
collating and using this information in the following way:

1. A simple questionnaire was drawn up (Appendix B) with
the intention of gaining basic information of a demographic sort
about the families being visited by caseworkers. The questionnaire was also designed to record a subjective assessment by
caseworkers of disturbance occurring amongst siblings in each
of their families. (The statistical data deriving from this is
presented separately in an appendix at the back of the book -
Appendix D.)

Questionnaires were then distributed amongst caseworkers,
one for each family they were visiting. Before filling them in,
however, all caseworkers attended a briefing session at which
the purpose of the questionnaire was explained. An attempt was
made to standardize the assessment of parental income, degree
of child's disability (see Appendix B) and disturbance among
siblings, by means of anchoring illustrations. In the case of
sibling disturbance, although it was hoped to achieve some degree
of uniformity regarding caseworkers' assessments, these assessments were only used as a starting point for more detailed discussion in the follow-up stage of the enquiry.

2. When all the questionnaires had been returned, I began a
series of tape-recorded interviews with each caseworker. The
purpose of this was threefold:

a. To clarify queries arising from the questionnaire.

b. To provide a check on the standardization of caseworkers' assessments.

c. To get away from simple value judgements about disturbance, towards an actual description of disturbed behaviour and
the family setting in which it is found.

The following questions were used as a framework for discussing each family:

a. Are the parents worried about the sibling? Do they think
of him as disturbed?

15

b.   How does the disturbance show? In what way is the
child's life affected?

c.   Have you talked to the child himself?

d.   Has the child ever been referred for 'treatment' e.g. to
a psychiatrist or child guidance clinic? If so what was the outcome?

e.   How does the child relate to the handicapped child?
And to other children?

f.   Does the presence of a handicapped child affect the
parents' relationship with this sibling? How? Does it affect
their relationship with each other? How?

g.   What are the parents' expectations of their respective
children?

h.   In what respects does their relationship with each child
differ?

These discussions with caseworkers provided a vast amount
of case material from which most of the illustrations in this book
were taken. As all of the discussions were recorded, I have
been able to quote from them verbatim. Occasionally the
material was supplemented by case reports from files and in
certain selected cases I visited the families in question myself.
This not only provided an opportunity to explore particular issues
more deeply with families, it also offered the chance to cross-
check, to some extent, the caseworker's assessment of the
situation. It was hoped as a result of all this to get an overall
picture of the sort of problems that siblings face, and also the
broad categories of family situation in which such problems arise.
While the study was in progress I also had my own caseload,
which meant that I was involved with a number of families and
their problems on a very intimate basis.

It is important to emphasize that although these procedures
were both devised and followed in as systematic a way as possible
- for they represent my chief means of access to the problems
I am describing - what follows in this book is not strictly speak-
ing the report of a research project. I have not, for example,
set out to test any particular hypothesis, nor do my illustrations
represent the carefully balanced outcome of a comprehensive
social survey. On the contrary, as a 'study' this book is essentially a distillation of my own professional experience of handicap, and as such it represents, as I have said, a personal point
of view.

In examining various issues, I have taken a variety of

different theoretical standpoints. In the chapter on family crisis, for example (chapter 5), I found it useful to employ the insights of role-theory, whereas at other times I have taken a distinctly psychoanalytic point of view. Clearly there are other, equally valid, standpoints which I could have taken in virtually every chapter. There is, for example, a wealth of both theory and fact about such things as family interaction, jealousy, aggression and bereavement and by no means all of it is represented in the respective chapters which deal with these things. What I have tried to do, however, is to select for each issue the standpoint which seems to me to be the most useful from a caseworker's point of view and to use it, not as a rigid structure by means of which a whole range of causal inferences and assumptions come into play, but rather as an aid to understanding, as a conceptual tool which enables us to structure our perception of certain situations in a way that gives them meaning.

My approach throughout has necessarily been general. The families I have described are made up of children of every age and background, having brothers and sisters who were handicapped in every imaginable way. The range of handicaps actually covered is listed in Appendix A. Because these siblings live in widely differing family environments and because they represent such a complete cross-section in terms of personality and social expectations, it is reasonable to ask whether they can meaningfully be treated as a group at all. I believe that they can, for there is, I believe, a tendency for certain patterns of relationship to be set up in families with a handicapped child; there is also a tendency for family interaction in all of these families to be put under largely similar sorts of strain.

Clearly, though, no matter how similar the situations they face, we must always remain cautious when treating siblings of the handicapped as any sort of homogeneous group. The impact of handicap on any given child is dependent on a whole host of variables and there is no way in which we can predict, for any child, just what this effect will be. Perhaps our best approach, therefore, is to regard the sibling as being exposed to a number of potential difficulties and problems. All we can hope to do here is to identify the potential areas of risk, and thus anticipate them in our roles as parents and professional agents of help.

3 Labelling children disturbed

This book is about the ways in which able-bodied children react to having a handicapped brother or sister. It concentrates specifically on those reactions which social workers in this field regard, for one reason or another, as being 'disturbed'.

Social workers do not have any monopoly on the use of this word disturbed. Psychiatrists, teachers, parents, paediatricians, judges and many other professional classes of people use it in the course of their work to describe certain children. What do they mean? How do children come to acquire such a label? What do those who acquire it have in common? Since the idea of disturbed behaviour underlies the selection of much of the material in this book, it is important to find answers to these questions, and in this chapter I would like to digress momentarily from the task of describing sibling disturbances, to consider some of the wider implications of using this word.

1. DIFFICULTY OF DEFINITION

Unfortunately it is not easy to define the concept of disturbance. Although some such concept is implicit in nearly every decision to refer a child, and in nearly every decision to offer 'treatment', it is nevertheless extremely hard to make general formulations about what disturbance is.

Some of the considerable difficulties involved in trying to formulate a global definition in this field can be illustrated by reference to the Underwood report. Underwood and his committee were concerned with the parallel problem of maladjustment, and after a great deal of deliberation they agreed that 'some system of classification, however inadequate, is necessary to make clear what are the characteristics of the children with whom we are concerned. All that can be attempted is a catalogue of the symptoms which children show'.

Accordingly they offer a lengthy list of symptoms which include the following:

1. Conditions following head injuries, encephalitis or cerebral tumours; epilepsy, chorea.

2. Unmanageableness - defiance, disobedience, refusal to go to work or school. Temper.

3. Stealing and begging. Truancy.

4. Unusual response to school discipline, bizzare symptoms.

5. Inability to concentrate. Apathy, lethargy, unresponsiveness, no interests.

6. For many of the symptoms listed, any and every manifestation does not indicate maladjustment, but only manifestations that are excessive or abnormal.

At another point in the report, however, the authors say that:

> 'Maladjustment is not a medical term diagnosing a medical condition (1). It is not to be equated with bad behaviour (2), delinquency (3), oddness (4), or educational subnormality (5), nor is it the same as deviation from the normal (6)'

These respective statements can be ironically compared with the previous list of 'symptoms'.

Underwood spent some time pointing out the pitfalls involved in making a global definition, but still felt in need of doing just that. The contradictions this led him into were endless and appear at times even in successive paragraphs:

> Para 88 'It (maladjustment) is not to be equated with bad behaviour.'
> Para 89 'In our view a child may be regarded as maladjusted who is developing in ways that have a bad effect on himself or his fellows.'

It is easy to point out such confusions, but not so easy to avoid them oneself. We are therefore faced with a serious drawback to the use of such words in the context of siblings. If disturbed behaviour is a particular sort of behaviour characterized by some qualitative difference from other sorts of behaviour, and if disturbed children do comprise a distinct class of child capable of classification by purely behavioural differences from other children, then surely we ought to be able to specify what these differences are, and thus derive a rule of observation by means of which we can distinguish disturbed from non-disturbed children. If, however, as Underwood's failure with maladjustment suggests, we cannot derive any such rule empirically, then we must surely question the meaning and use of the concept of disturbance.

What I shall argue in this chapter is that the idea of disturbance means different things to different people. It varies from one psychiatrist and social worker to the next and from one cultural group to another. Practitioners have widely differing views about the sort of function they are supposed to fulfil as professional people; they use differing concepts for understanding the behaviour of the child, differing standards for evaluating the normality of his behaviour, and differing methods for treating his abnormalities.

Children come to be labelled disturbed for a variety of reasons, therefore, and the fact that they are so labelled does not necessarily mean that they have anything in common with one another. In practice we cannot distinguish disturbed children from non-disturbed children in the same way that we can distinguish children with anaemia or chicken-pox from those who are healthy. We can learn a lot about how a particular child has come to be called disturbed, but there is at present no universally acceptable rule according to which the label should be applied.

It is for this reason that any study employing the concept of disturbance must be very careful to examine its use of the word. It is for this reason, also, that the conceptual problems raised in this chapter are important even for the practising worker who is 'out in the field'. For until we have struggled with the difficulties of defining it, we cannot realize just how often our day to day assessments of behaviour as disturbed are based on our own personal values and biases and not, as we may prefer to imagine, on any strictly empirical or self-evident criteria.

To the person involved in professional practice, the definition of general terms often seems to be less useful than the ability to identify recognized patterns of behaviour. Thus the social worker or teacher is able to recognize the sort of child he has learnt to regard as disturbed, and in any particular case he can usually give reasons for the application of this label which are sufficient to satisfy other members of his profession. However, he may not, if pressed, be able to say what the label actually means, and he is unlikely to be able to support his assessment by reference to any general criteria of disturbance.

The fact that he can get away with this does not mean that his use of the term is beyond reproach. Indeed it is precisely because the average practitioner is never called upon to define the use of the label that it is so often applied arbitrarily, inconsistently, and with connotations which are quite unfair to the child.

To look for disturbance amongst siblings of the disabled, we must clearly have in mind some general idea of what disturbance is. In examining some of the confusions and inconsistencies to which I have referred, then, I shall be working towards an examination of the particular concept of disturbance which has governed the selection of material for this book.

2. CONCEPTUAL CONFUSIONS

A label such as 'disturbed' has many possible meanings and connotations, yet it is often applied without specifying exactly which of these is intended. Once applied, it is all too easy for originally unintended meanings and connotations to be tagged on to a child along with the label. Examples of confused and loose thinking about the use of this label abound. It is commonplace, for example, for authors to use 'maladjusted', 'deviant', 'disordered', 'delinquent', 'maladaptive' and 'abnormal' as synonyms for 'disturbed', and many of these variants can be found in the literature on siblings.

Kellmer Pringle, Butler and Davis (1966) for example, in the report of the National Child Development Study, use different tests for rating 'maladjustment' and 'disturbance' for seven-year-old children. But despite this, the distinction between the two is never made clear on a conceptual level and there are a number of occasions when they are used as alternative terms for a single idea (e.g. p.108).

D.H. Stott (1956) talks of 'unsettled', 'maladjusted', 'unhappy' and 'abnormal' children on a single page (p.43) as if all four words were identical, and many more examples of the failure to distinguish between such terms may be found in the Report of the Committee on Maladjusted Children (1955). Sentences such as the following occur throughout the Report:

'Maladjustment does not always show itself in aggressive or troublesome conduct, indeed, quiet and passive behaviour may overlay deep emotional disturbance.'

Do we infer from such usage that 'maladjustment' and 'emotional disturbance' are the same? Furthermore are either or both of these the same as 'abnormal', 'delinquent' or 'deviant'? Kellmer Pringle in a follow-up report ('Policy Implications of Child Development Studies' in Concern, no. 3, November 1969), gives us an indication of what emotional disturbance means to her in terms of symptoms:

'(It) shows itself in such behaviour as destructiveness, inability to settle to anything for more than a few minutes, and being unduly upset by new situations.'

It is interesting to note that the same three factors were considered by Glueck to have a high predictive value for 'delinquent' children. So here we might also infer that, for this age group at least, 'emotional disturbance' is symptomatically the same as 'delinquency'.

It is possible to minimize confusion of this sort by using one word alone and ignoring the fact that a choice has been made. But quite apart from other objections, this often leads to a strangely inappropriate use of labels. Blau and Hulse (1956) for example opt for the use of 'behaviour disorder', and they describe in the following way the sort of behaviour they have in mind when they use this term:

'In the behaviour disorder one sees that the child has not submitted with a sense of failure and helplessness but is fighting to save himself as an individual, despite the tremendous odds that he faces. The opposition is in many ways fantastic, unrealistic and futile, but it still means that he has not given up.'

The authors here seem to be unaware of a fundamental contradiction between their description of the child's behaviour and the name with which they label it. One might legitimately argue from their description that any other behaviour on the part of the child would be a 'dis-order', and as Lindy Burton (1968) points out, it is equally inappropriate to call such behaviour 'maladaptive'. What then can we call it? 'Disturbed' seems in many ways a more innocuous term, but is this perhaps because it is simply more general and imprecise?

To raise such a host of questions about labels is not just being pedantic, for although the different words I have listed often appear to be interchangeable they do in fact assume a wide range of different meanings.

Confusion seems to arise from the fact that despite their range of meaning, the respective words may all be used in any particular case to describe the same child or the same behavioural act. What we are inclined to overlook is that although the referrent of these terms is the same, the function each word performs vis a vis the child and his behaviour can vary. For example, the term 'maladjusted' can be used to express a certain sort of relationship between the child and his social environment, whereas 'disturbed' can denote a condition which is assessed purely in terms of the internal dynamics of the child. Thus, the two words can function in quite different ways even though they might be used to describe the selfsame acts of behaviour.

Unfortunately, the situation is further confused by the fact that each of the words we have looked at has by itself not one but a number of possible functions. The word 'disturbed' alone has at least seven (there may well be more), and these I have listed below. This means that there are at least seven different ways of using this word, each of which involves a different conceptual orientation. Some of the synonym words may have other possible functions, but, perhaps unfortunately, all of them can be used to function in at least some of the ways that 'disturbance' is commonly used. It is not surprising, then, that these words and their meanings are frequently confused.

MEANINGS OF DISTURBANCE	
'Disturbance' may denote:	Conceptual orientation underlying these uses
1. An undesirable mental state or pattern of behaviour	Based on value judgement of what is desirable and what isn't
2. A collection of symptoms signifying impairment of functioning in some aspect of life	Based on the concept of 'dis-order'
3. Deviation from normal (average) behaviour	Based on statistical norms

Table continued overleaf

'Disturbance' may denote:	Conceptual orientation underlying these uses
4. A social process inferred from a wide range of factors, e.g. deprivation leads to disturbance	Based on personal case-history, and inferred from certain antecedents
5. An arbitrary social description, e.g. all children who attend child-guidance clinics, etc.	Based on formal or demographic criteria
6. The need for 'treatment' or 'intervention'	Based on pragmatic criteria and specific agency functions
7. An inference from questionnaire or other secondary sources	Based on psychological inventory and consensus on the meaning of scores

3. SUBSTANTIVE PROBLEMS

The confusions I have looked at so far have been purely linguistic in nature. They are, in other words, confusions about the way in which 'disturbance' is being used. It is possible, however, to agree on the way in which this word is being used, but to disagree, often quite radically, on what is and what is not in actual fact a manifestation of disturbance. Disagreement of this sort raises issues which are substantive rather than linguistic in nature.

Most of the meanings in the list, 3, 5, 6 and 7 for example, imply the use of some secondary and often quite arbitrary data (as specified in the right hand column) against which any assessment of disturbance may be clearly validated. If we are using the word in sense number 7, for example, the validity of any given assessment can be checked against the disturbance score given to the child in the particular test he completed. If his score indicates disturbance by exceeding a predetermined amount, the fact will be obvious to everyone, though even then we can only call the child disturbed in relation to his score on this particular test, and we have no grounds for assuming that because he is disturbed in this strictly prescribed sense, he is necessarily disturbed in any of the other senses listed. To say that a child is disturbed in this case, then, would mean no more than that he obtained a particular score on a particular test at a given moment in time.

Clearly for this sort of usage there will be no disagreement over the validity of any given assessment and therefore the substantive problem does not arise. (Unless, that is, we choose to question the criteria of disturbance which are implicit in the construction of the test being used.)

Usually, however, in a social work situation, 'disturbance' is not used in such a specific way, its more open and ambiguous meanings, such as 2 and 4 in the list, being the most common. For meanings such as this there are no simple criteria against which we can reliably validate any given assessment. If two social workers disagree as to whether or not a given child is disturbed in this global sense, there is at present no way in which we can decide which of the two is right.

It is tempting to think that in day to day practice social workers and other professionals just do not disagree over such matters. Indeed I have heard it said on a number of occasions that when one comes across a child who really is disturbed, this fact will be immediately obvious to a person with professional training. Needless to say, such naive faith in professional skill masks significant areas of dissent both in individual assessments and in general formulations about disturbance.

It is clearly important to examine this dissent, not with the intention of discrediting professional judgement but simply to ascertain the true status of the label 'disturbed'.

Are there such things as symptoms of disturbance?

The disorder concept of disturbance (meaning 2 and 4 on the list) rests on the assumption that certain forms of behaviour constitute symptoms. As one textbook puts it

'We shall start with the facts - the events to be explained - and then proceed to an understanding of these events. The "events" of psychopathology consist of symptoms. Once we know what the symptoms are, we can proceed to the theories that attempt to explain them'.

In this approach, the presence of certain symptoms is held to be indicative of disturbance in the person, or alternatively, the symptom may itself be regarded as the disturbance; thus we talk of disturbed behaviour as well as disturbed people.

Now this sort of approach is fine just so long as there is a clear consensus about the sort of behaviour that constitutes a symptom, rather than being just normal. But as I have suggested, and as the quotation from Underwood confirms, very little meaningful consensus has been reached in this respect. Indeed there is no real agreement as yet over how behaviour can be classified into 'sorts', let alone over which sorts are disturbed and which are not. As a result the whole idea of a behavioural symptom is lacking in empirical validity as well as in conceptual clarity.

Nowhere are differences of opinion about symptoms more apparent than in the field of childhood and adolescence; one reason for this is that most 'normal' adolescents behave in ways which in other contexts would probably be regarded as 'disturbed'. The question that arises here, then, is whether we should label all normal adolescents as 'disturbed', or somehow bend the rules of definition and say that in their case the 'symptoms' they display are not a sign of real disturbance.

The professional reaction to such a question is mixed. Spiegel, for example, is one of many who has pointed out (in 1951 and 1961) the resemblance of adolescence to certain psychotic episodes. He cites withdrawal, broodiness, promiscuity, and certain forms of aggression, as 'symptoms' which are common to both 'conditions'. I.B. Weiner is another who, at the end of a long and detailed study (1970), maintains that if a symptom is being displayed at all, it cannot be regarded 'benignly' as part of a developmental phase, but on the contrary warrants as much professional concern and attention in an adolescent as it would in an adult.

In direct contrast to this sort of approach, Anna Freud talks of the symptoms of adolescent disturbance as 'the external indications that normal developmental internal adjustments are taking place.'

Gardner (1947) says:

'It is my feeling and my experience that 90 per cent of the so-called 'problems' of adolescents have to do with normal reactions or normal phases through which the adolescent passes in his journey toward adulthood.'

and Geleerd (1957) completely reverses Weiner's dictum when he says:

'Personally I would feel greater concern for the adolescent
who causes no trouble and feels no disturbance.'

There are, of course, others who sit cautiously on the fence and
take an intermediate position. Sprince (1964), for example,
says:

'It is only when a developmental reconstruction can be made
in the course of diagnosis and therapy that a clear distinction
between pathology and the normal adolescent process can be
attempted.'

But cautious wording and compromise of this sort tends to hide
rather than resolve the central issue. This issue is, how can
we decide objectively whether or not an adolescent, or anyone
else for that matter, is disturbed. And in the case of the
adolescent, so long as our putative 'symptoms' can be seen to
consist in perfectly 'normal' behaviour, it seems that the question
will continue to go unanswered. What, after all, is the point of
viewing normal behaviour as a disorder?

As the above quotations indicate, the professionals are a
long way from reaching a consensus about what is and what isn't
a symptom of disturbance. Certainly it is not just a question of
recognizing any clearly distinguishable forms of behaviour. For
a start, human behaviour just does not yield to simple forms of
classification. And secondly, even when there is agreement on
the sort of behaviour in question, there is still disagreement
over whether or not it is 'normal' as opposed to 'disturbed'.

Things would be easier if adolescence were a special case,
the exception to a general rule, but in reality it is not. In point
of fact virtually every form of behaviour that one could call a
symptom of disturbance is essentially normal, in the fullest
sense of that word. We have only to return to Underwood's list
to see the truth of this. What normal child, after all, has not
felt anger, aggression, jealousy and defiance? And what normal
child has not been unresponsive or lethargic or disobedient at
times? Yet these normal forms of behaviour were the only
symptoms of maladjustment that Underwood could name.

There is altogether a great deal of evidence to suggest that
the concept of a symptom of disturbance is not workable in
practice. It was shown by Slotkin, for example, that what is
thought of as a symptom in one society is not always considered
to be such in others (1959). And Tindall, who compared five
different methods of assessing disturbance which are currently

being used in this country, concluded that there was so little agreement about what was and wasn't a manifestation of disturbed behaviour, that global assessments of this sort had no real empirical meaning (1959). His results showed that there was no significant relation between the various methods he tested. In other words, persons who were rated disturbed by one method would not necessarily be rated disturbed by the others.

It seems, therefore, on the basis of all the evidence, that we can use the term disturbed in strictly prescribed senses, such as 3 and 5 in the list, but we simply cannot use it in a generic way as if we have made some meaningful empirical classification.

What, then, is disturbance?

Although the facts I have presented so far may lead us to think blithely in terms of doing away with the idea of disturbance, and although it is clearly evasive as an empirical concept, it is one that we cannot easily avoid, even though we might wish to do so.

Quite apart from any specialized meaning which professionals may attach to it, the idea of being disturbed is deeply rooted in the day to day vocabulary of ordinary people. We feel disturbed by the state of the world, by events around us, by art, theatre and film. We feel disturbed by personal disaster and loss, such as the death of a friend or the misfortune of one of the family. An unexpected train of events or the upsurge within us of feelings we cannot explain or control leaves us as individuals feeling disturbed.

When we think of disturbance in this everyday sense rather than as an exact empirical label, a number of significant changes occur in our thinking. For a start we no longer think of it as a psychological disorder. After all, there is nothing inherently wrong with a person who feels disturbed by the death of a friend or loved one. It is not unnatural or abnormal; on the contrary such 'disturbance' is an integral part of our everyday existence, even though it may contain elements of unpleasantness or pain.

The second change which occurs is that we no longer think of disturbance as a type of behaviour which can be classified according to symptoms; we think of it more as a mode of personal experience.

This represents a significant change of perspective, for when we say that we feel deeply disturbed by an event, we are no longer

trying to make an exact classification of a psychological state;
we are instead using broad and figurative language to describe
the way we subjectively feel.

The still surface of the pool of our experience is broken by
an ill wind: we feel disturbed. The delicate balance between
security and separation, confidence and fear, dependence and
vulnerability is suddenly upset; we are beset by catastrophe,
by the unexpected, the unknown, by forces of destruction against
which we have insufficient power to fight: we feel at such times
that the steady balance of our lives has been disturbed. This is
hardly the language of science, but it is precisely here that the
mistake has crept in, for we are not in fact dealing with the
language of science but with the subjective language of experience.
When we try to objectify experience we find that the metaphors
through which it speaks break down, the edges grow blurred and
indistinct, their meaning drains away.

I would suggest that this is precisely what has happened in
our search for a definition of disturbance. The idea we have
been juggling with is essentially a figure of speech describing
our experience of certain situations. It cannot be translated
from this metaphorical form to cover a discrete class of
behaviour or a certain type of person.

It is not surprising, then, that reliable definitions and
accurate methods of classification have eluded us. When we say
that a child is disturbed we are not classifying a definitive
condition from which he is suffering, we are merely reaching
out to his experience of himself and of the world in which he lives.

It should be obvious that language of this order cannot simply
be erased from everyday use. It will also, I hope, be clear that
the act of reaching out in an effort to enter another person's
world is something that we cannot afford to ignore either on a
professional or a personal level. To empathise with the disturbed
experience of the other is the first step in every helping relationship. Only when we have seen and acknowledged the nature of
the other person's experience of life are we in a position to work
out what has gone wrong for him and thus to explore all the
possible avenues of help. For this reason, I believe it is
important to retain the notion of disturbance, provided, that is,
we don't let it lead us astray as a label.

In many ways the concept of disturbance is like the concept
of intelligence which, as Arnold Buss says, 'has great practical
significance, but little scientific stature'. We would do best to

regard it, therefore, as a rough everyday notion - an essential part of our vocabulary of the emotions, but devoid of theoretical pretensions.

This, at any rate, is how I have used it in this study. In describing reactions and responses which indicate that the child's life and emotions are disturbed, I have not tried to distinguish rigidly between normal reactions and abnormal ones, between disturbance as a natural phenomenon and disturbance as a disorder. If there is a dividing line between the two it is surely a pragmatic one in the sense that certain children appear to be more in need of help and attention than others. As I hope I have shown, it certainly cannot be based on the presence of any symptoms that set the latter group apart.

I am well aware that not everyone would agree with this standpoint. Some of the caseworkers I spoke to, for example, took the attitude that a child who 'takes everything in his stride' and appears unruffled by inherently disturbing events must be denying his feelings and should therefore be regarded as disturbed, whereas the attention-seeking child who verbalizes his feelings of aggression towards his handicapped sibling should be regarded as healthily normal. At first sight this may seem an odd reversal of logic, but it is clearly determined by an idea of what is and what is not a 'normal' response in an inherently stressful situation.

Rightly or wrongly, I have chosen not to distinguish between normal and abnormal reactions in this way, partly on the grounds that any distinction of this sort must of necessity be arbitrary, and partly because to do so would serve very little practical purpose.

What I have done, in fact, is to regard any disturbed reaction, in the everyday sense of this word, whether reputedly normal or not, as worthy of description. To this end I have merely tried to identify the main sources of stress for the siblings of the disabled, and to describe the most common ways in which they react to, and cope with, such stress.

This approach raises the question of how we can be sure whether the disturbed reactions we find are related to the presence of a handicapped child or whether they would have occurred anyway? After all, when one is looking for disturbances in any sample of children one can all too easily find them. Why should we assume, therefore, that any disturbance amongst siblings of the disabled are necessarily related to disability?

In reply to this question, it should be noted first of all that I have tried not to make this assumption. I have in fact tried to distinguish between those sorts of disturbed experience and behaviour which appear to be specifically related to handicap and those where there is little or no evidence to suggest a connection of this sort. Clearly there is still a problem in deciding what is and is not legitimate evidence of a connection, though it may be noted that the relation between the presence of a handicapped child and many of the disturbances I shall describe is implicit in the very nature of the disturbance itself. There can be no doubt, for example, that the child who lives in fear of hospitals following the hospitalization of his handicapped brother, or the girl who is afraid that her own children will be handicapped when she grows up, or the child who is ashamed to be seen in the street with his handicapped sibling, each face a problem which is unquestionably posed by handicap. Similarly for many other sorts of difficulty facing siblings, we shall see that the so-called disturbance is expressed in a way that leaves no room for doubt about its source.

But apart from the more obvious cases like these it must be admitted that the link between disturbed behaviour in the sibling and the effect of a handicapped child on the family, may at times be no more than an unjustified assumption of psychological cause and effect on the part of the caseworker or myself. The only reply to such a charge in the absence of clear-cut proof is that the 'assumed link' arose in the first place not from guess-work or theory, but from repeated observations on family visits, and perhaps more important than this, from talking with siblings themselves.

References

Blau, A. and Hulse, W. Anxiety neurosis as a cause of behaviour disorders in children. 'American J. of Orthopsychiatry'. vol. 26, 1956, pp 108-118.

Burton, L. 'Vulnerable Children'. Routledge, 1968.

Buss, A. 'Psychopathology'. Wiley, New York, 1966.

Freud, A. 'Normality and Pathology in Childhood'. Hogarth Press, 1966.

Gardner, G.E.   'The mental health of normal adolescents'.
Mental Hygiene, 31, 1947, pp 529-540.

Geleerd, E.   'Some aspects of psychoanalytic technique in
adolescence'.   'Psychoanalytic Study of the Child', 12, 1957,
pp 263-283.

Gluck, I. and Wrenn, M.   'Contributions to the Understanding of
Disturbances'.   'Brit. J. of Med. Psychiatry', vol. 32,
1959, p. 171.

Glueck, S. and Glueck, E.   'Family Environment and
Delinquency'.   Routledge and Kegan Paul, 1962.

Kellmer Pringle, M.   'Policy Implications of Child Development
Studies'.   'Concern', no. 3, November 1969.

Kellmer Pringle, M., Butler, N. and Davie, R.   '11,000 Seven
Year Olds'.   First Report of the National Child Development
Study.   Longmans, 1966.

Masterson, J.F.   'The Psychiatric Dilemma of Adolescence'.
Boston, 1967.

Masterson, J.F.   'The Psychiatric Significance of Adolescent
Turmoil'.   'American Journal of Psychiatry', 124, 1968,
pp 1549-1554.

Slotkin, J.S.   'Culture and Psychopathology'.   In 'Readings in
the Psychology of Adjustment',   L. Gurlow and W. Katovsky
(Eds).   New York, 1959.

Spiegel, L.   A review of contributions to a psychoanalytic theory
of adolescence.   'Psychoanalytic Study of the Child', 6,
1951, pp 375-393.

Spiegel, L.   'Disorder and consolidation in adolescence'.
'Journal of the Amer. Psychoanalytic Ass.', 9, 1961,
pp 406-417.

Sprince, M.   'A contribution to the study of homosexuality in
adolescence'.   'J. of Child Psychol. and Psychiatry', 5,
1964, pp 103-117.

Stott, D.H.   'Unsettled Children and their Families'.
University of London Press, 1956.

· Labelling children disturbed

Tindall, R.H. 'Relation between measures of adjustment'. In
    'Readings in the Psychology of Adjustment', L. Gurlow and
    W. Katovsky (Eds). New York, 1959.

Underwood, J. Report of the Committee on Maladjusted
    Children. HMSO, 1955.

Valentine, C.W. 'The Normal Child'. Pelican, 1962.

Weiner, I.B. 'Psychological Disturbance in Adolescence'.
    Wiley, 1970.

4 Parental reactions to the birth of a handicapped child

'It should be emphasised that because child and family are part of one another it is in no way possible in a clinical estimate to disassociate child from family.'

Nathan Ackerman.

Young children have limited resources for coping with frightening or threatening experiences. When they are faced with danger, they instinctively turn to their parents who act as an intermediary between themselves and the source of the threat – it is largely from their parents that children learn what is to be feared and what is not to be feared, what is an appropriate response and what is an inappropriate response, in strange or stressful situations.

We must therefore come to grips not only with the immediate effect that the handicapped child has on his siblings, but with the effect he has on his parents, for this will determine what changes, if any, take place in the relationship between sibling and parent, as well as affecting the sibling's attitudes to handicap in general.

Changes in the relationship between themselves and their parents are far more important for siblings than the mere presence in the family of a handicapped child – especially when such changes are caused by factors beyond their own power of control. Furthermore, disturbances in childhood cannot be classified and understood simply in terms of the individual child's behaviour. If we hope to come to terms with, or to change, the behaviour we regard as 'disturbed', it is necessary to under-stand the social dynamics which underlie it. In other words, we can only realistically assess the child's experience and behaviour in the context of what is happening in his primary environment: home. If we do not do this we will fail to understand his 'disturb-ance' except on the shallowest of levels.

· Parental reactions to the birth of a handicapped child

In this section, then, I would like to consider some of the
ways in which parents commonly react and adjust to the birth of
a handicapped child, before turning my attention to the siblings
themselves.

All families are unique, and parental reactions are bound to
vary in some respects from one family to the next, no matter
how similar the experiences they undergo. There are certain
aspects of the emotional response of parents to the birth of a
handicapped child, however, which are so common as to be almost
universal, and it is these which I would like to examine in the
present chapter. In the next chapter I shall outline some of the
consequences of these responses, and look at the ways in which
different aspects of family functioning may be affected. Taken
together these two parts should provide a pointer to the family
backcloth (vis a vis the issue of handicap), against which the
disturbances and problems of siblings may be viewed.

THE MEANING OF AN ABNORMAL BIRTH

Some authorities (e.g. Caplan 1961 and Lomas 1967) regard
pregnancy itself as a period of susceptibility to crisis. It is
hardly surprising, therefore, that when a normal pregnancy
results in the birth of a child who is impaired, a crisis almost
inevitably ensues. As with all human crises, this sort of event
does not exist in a vacuum. Parents who are going to have a baby
will have had many feelings and thoughts about the meaning of
this event in their lives. They will have developed an image
(albeit a vague one, and one which did not perhaps arise out of
conscious processes of thought, but an image nevertheless) of the
sort of child they expect. It is against this expectation of normal
birth, that the initial crisis of handicap should be seen.

Normal expectations

The meaning of childbirth varies enormously from one parent
to the next. Ackerman points out that

> 'some women have an intense desire for a child, some crave
> many, some few, some do not want any. Some want a child
> not for the love of the child but for some ulterior motive; to
> neutralize anxiety concerning frigidity or sterility; to please
> or punish the husband; to use as a pawn in the parental
> conflict; to keep a marriage "off the rocks"; to win the

the approval of other persons, grandparents or women friends; to fulfil a conventional idealized image of family life; to make into a parent figure; to use as a symbol of the suffering of the female; to mould into a more perfect edition of self; to live vicariously through the child; to make the child into a masculine, aggressive extension of oneself, or to give the child what the mother herself never had in her childhood.'

It should be clear without extending this list that not all parents desire a child for the sake of the child himself. Some desire the child as a defence against their own feelings of inadequacy, others as a defence against the break-up of the family. If the child turns out to be handicapped, the nature of the parent's reaction will, in part, depend upon which of these expectations is at work.

Despite such a variety of motives for childbirth, however, there are once again certain needs and expectations which are so common as to be almost universal amongst parents awaiting the arrival of a child. Three in particular deserve mention here.

a. Parents expect a normal child. It is not by mistake that pregnant women are said to be 'expectant'. They expect not merely 'a child' in the abstract, but rather the particular child who is present as an image in their minds, and no matter how many irrational fears they may have of something going wrong, for all but a few the image they have of their baby will be something of an ideal; normal, healthy and without any defects or peculiarities. Plans may be made on the basis of such an ideal; expectations may be developed of family life and growth in which the parents can put into practice their conceptions of good parenthood. These expectations almost inevitably undergo some modification when the image in the mind is transformed into a reality in the world. But in cases where the child turns out to be deformed, there is an enormous discrepancy between image and reality. This discrepancy can be so great that the parents find themselves, at least temporarily, without the resources to cope with the reality they face.

b. Parents seek creative fulfilment. Not only do parents have the expectation of producing a 'normal' healthy child, they also feel the need to create something which is good. Childbirth is the archetypal act of creation. The birth of a healthy child inspires a feeling of virility in the male and a sense of wholeness and wellbeing in the woman. It is an outward visible manifestation of the life which is within. Winnicott realized this when he said:

'a girl who longs for a baby to some extent longs for the
reassurance that she has taken something good, has retained
it and has something good developing inside her. This is a
reassurance she needs (though it is a false one) because of her
unconscious feeling that she may be empty, or full of bad
things.'

Childbirth is not merely the creation of another being, therefore,
for in a very real sense, it is themselves that parents 'reproduce'
when they bring a child into the world. This fact may be threatening to some parents and pleasing to others, but it is always
significant when the child in question is born deformed. The
feeling of being 'empty and full of bad things' is one to which we
will later return.

    c. Parents seek continuity of lineage. The importance of
this factor - and it is perhaps more important for men than
woman - is well illustrated by the attention it has received in
literature throughout the world. Not all childless parents pray
to God with the same fervour as Abraham and Sarah, but when a
couple have conceived, the sense of personal continuity, and the
pride which this engenders, certainly take their part in shaping
the meaning of the birth they await. A severe congenital disorder
in the child can extinguish this pride, and might render impossible
the chance of ever extending the family line.

    These needs and expectations are some of the most basic to
affect the parent-to-be. There are doubtless many others which
could be mentioned here, as Ackerman's list suggests, but
parents will vary a great deal as to which of these affect them,
and in the degree to which they are affected. It is worth remember-
ing that people do not respond directly to external events. They
respond to the internal meanings which those events take on.
Such meanings may be highly complex, drawing on experience
which dates back for many years, and on expectations which have
been built up over a lifetime. Nevertheless, the particular meaning of childbirth to any individual parent must be thoroughly
explored if we wish to understand their subsequent reaction to
the news that their child is retarded or disabled. For in the crisis
that results when this is found to be so, the crucial element is
not the disorder itself, but the demolition of existing parental
expectations.

THE CRISIS

It is time to look at the structure of this crisis in a little more detail. According to Caplan, 'a crisis is what happens when a person faces a difficulty, either a threat of loss, or a loss, in which his existing coping repertoire is insufficient, and he therefore has no immediate way of handling the stress.' This seems to be a useful way of regarding what happens to parents when they are told that their new-born baby is deformed.

They find themselves in a situation where it is suddenly necessary to make enormous practical and psychological adjustments on a variety of different fronts. It is true that we are all continually adjusting to the changing realities of the world, but in everyday life this process is slow and situations are usually manageable, so that the mature individual can adjust to them without losing his mental and emotional balance. In the situation we are considering here, however, the demand for adjustment is sudden. Parents find that their whole range of expectations and assumptions about parenthood is proved in one stroke to be at odds with reality. The situation they face is therefore to a large extent outside their existing frame of reference. Because it is also likely to be very painful, they will usually find some way of defending themselves against it.

The form which their defence takes does not seem to vary very much from one parent to the next. It was pointed out by R.D. Laing that 'the official dates of public events can be out of phase with the structure of experience', and this is exactly what happens in the present context. Because parents are initially unable to handle the stress, there is often a time-lag between the event itself and the date at which the event becomes an emotional reality. The doctor may make a clear and unequivocal medical diagnosis, leaving no room for doubt about the child's condition and future prospects, yet in emotional terms his diagnosis may not be accepted by parents for weeks, months, or even years. They know what the doctor has said, but they do not feel it to be true. Perhaps they do not feel it to be true because to do so would be painful and disruptive, and they do not want to experience disruption and pain. Perhaps they are frightened or overwhelmed by the implications of the truth. Whichever is the case, social workers who work with these parents during their time of distress would say that their equilibrium has not been restored until they are able to accept on an emotional level the truth of what has happened.

· Parental reactions to the birth of a handicapped child

Acceptance in this sense has nothing to do with being meek
and mild in the face of adversity, or for that matter with the
decision to keep the child at home rather than send him to an
institution. Acceptance, as I use it here, refers to the point at
which parents no longer feel impelled to defend themselves
against the truth, and against their own experience of pain.
The time-lag between the event and the emotional acceptance
of the event embodies two distinct reactions.

Shock

The first reaction of any parent is inevitably one of numbness
and shock. This is particularly marked when the news is broken
by a doctor who is tactless or in a hurry, or by one who has
failed to prepare the parents adequately for what he has to say.
The shock-reaction of numbness is a primitive method of
shielding oneself from pain; it acts as an immediate though
temporary anaesthetic which allows the mind time to construct
a more adequate system of defence. Parents in this state tend
to live in a daze, unable to respond realistically to the people
or things around them. They may repeat over and over again
such things as 'I can't believe this has happened' or 'Why did
it happen to me?' or simply, 'I don't understand.' Social
workers have noticed that it is no use offering advice, or
attempting to 'talk things out' with parents at this stage as the
condition is basically a withdrawal from, and an immunity to,
the threat of the outside world. It is sadly ironic that the time
when parents suffer from severe shock and are most withdrawn
is the very time when their children most need to come close to
them, and feel their reassurance, and yet are least likely to be
able to do so.

Denial

Shock-reaction is something of a passive, short-lived resistance;
more active and enduring is the process of denial which frequently
follows it. Denial is quite simply the refusal to accept the truth,
in the sense of 'acceptance' referred to above. 'This is the case'
becomes 'this is not the case'. Doctor declares 'your child is
handicapped'; parent protests 'my child is not handicapped'. One
mother I knew who responded in this way put her severely
retarded son down for a place at a public school, even though she

39

knew that he would never be able to read or write.

As one might expect, there are degrees of denial. Not every parent will refute their doctor's judgement outright, for they usually feel in their hearts that there is something wrong with their child. Most, however, will disbelieve it on some level. A letter sent by a confused and frightened mother to an American doctor, Abraham Levinson, illustrates the painful way in which denial and realization frequently co-exist. This mother writes:

> 'All the doctors told us that our little girl is mongoloid and that she will never grow mentally, but we just can't believe they are right. She does have a look about her eyes though, that kind of worries us, they're slanty like. And sometimes we even think she may be blind, because she doesn't respond or smile like most babies of her age. There is something we feel, but we pray that the doctors are wrong.'

It is not hard to understand why such parents 'shop around' from one doctor to the next, hoping that somewhere along the line they will be offered a diagnosis that is easier to bear. Many of them confront nurses, friends and relatives in a desperate search for someone who will collude with their own wishful thinking; people who are too polite or embarrassed to be entirely truthful can usually be found to provide fodder for such thinking.

Some of these parents may draw hope from stories of miraculous cures, others may try to assert their will over the child, perhaps using their physical strength to 'combat' his spasms, or calling forth all their mental resources in an effort to 'will him to be normal'. Eventually, however, a more realistic attitude is bound to force itself upon them, though this does not mean of course that all their problems will suddenly disappear. On the contrary, it is only when they can see how things really are that the difficulties of re-adjusting can properly be faced. Let us look briefly at some of the painful emotions with which parents must cope.

Grief

A natural reaction which most parents experience at some stage or other is the feeling of profound grief. Different writers have characterized this reaction in various ways. Simon Olshansky refers to it as a 'pervasive psychological reaction of chronic sorrow', and he stresses the importance of recognizing

Parental reactions to the birth of a handicapped child

this factor for all those who attempt to help families with
severely handicapped children. The grief that parents feel is
likened by some social workers to the normal process of mourn-
ing, and it may well be related to the loss, and metaphorical
'death' of the child they expected.

Anxiety, fright, horror

Mothers who get together in groups run by the ICAA often discuss
the feelings of revulsion they sometimes have for their handicapped children. It is quite common for these feelings to give
rise at times to death-wishes, which intrude into their consciousness in an uncontrollable way. Such feelings can be very strong
and parents are understandably alarmed and frightened by them.
Because they are frightened by the strength of their feelings, the
feelings themselves tend to get pushed out of mind and repressed.
The conflict thus generated causes the mother to become generally
more anxious, and she may also feel extremely guilty at having
entertained such thoughts in the first place.
      Both grief and anxiety are peculiarly infectious emotions and
it has long been known how easily they are transmitted to a child
by its mother or mother-substitute. Even inexplicable and
irrational anxieties can be transmitted to siblings with the utmost
rapidity; when such feelings persist over a long period of time,
as they frequently do, their effect on siblings cannot lightly be
dismissed.

Guilt

The arousal of feelings of guilt is another parental reaction that
is almost inevitable. Right up until the turn of the last century
the association between deformity and guilt was not only widespread but also quite socially acceptable: deformity in the child
was a sign of divine retribution for the guilt of the parent. Even
today this attitude persists, though the religious component is
frequently missing. Time and again parents feel that their own
ambivalence towards sex, towards their marital partner, or
'flaws' in their own personality are responsible for the deformity
of their child. These associations are quite irrational, but they
can be extremely deep-rooted. We may recall Winnicott's
observation that many people unconsciously feel they are 'empty
or full of bad things'.

Such feelings are suddenly confirmed in a stark and apparently incontrovertible way by the arrival of a deformed child.

Shame

The sense of guilt is triggered by 'internal' associations; the corresponding feeling of shame is externally triggered. Most mothers love nothing better than to compare the development of their child with that of other children, and when a group of mothers gets together it is only a matter of time before the conversation comes round to this subject. Fathers, too, take a natural pride in watching the physical and mental development of their child. When this development is stunted both parents are therefore vulnerable to acute embarrassment and shame whenever they are with other people. Some children, such as mongols, exaggerate this vulnerability by being extremely forthright and spontaneous with strangers in a way that would be embarrassing at the best of times, and this draws even more attention to their abnormality. It is not surprising that many parents try to hide away their handicapped children, often by 'hiding away' themselves and becoming extremely isolated from friends and relatives. One family I visited felt so ashamed of their spastic child that for three years they were unable to tell the maternal grandparents, with whom they had kept in regular postal contact, that there was anything wrong with the child.

Shame is often associated with the label of handicap. Many parents of the mentally retarded, for example, will admit that their child is 'just a little slow', but will strive desperately hard to avoid the label of retardation. One questionnaire survey in Australia showed that this is particularly true for families who are socially mobile in an upward direction.

There are many other emotional responses which could be mentioned here: for example the confusion and ignorance that parents inevitably feel when they are faced with a baby who is so different that they need special medical and child-care knowledge to look after him properly; the continued frustration of rearing a child who is incontinent or in need of constant attention, or one whose condition presents a behaviour problem; the depression which so many parents go through. One should perhaps mention, however, that these negative emotions are a response to the negative aspects of handicap, and although these are likely to

prevail initially, and often for a very long period of time, it
should be remembered that when all is said and done the handicapped child is still a child. These negative emotions will therefore not be unmixed with the normal joys of childbirth.

UNDERSTANDING THE PARENTS' REACTION

So far I have examined the parental response to handicap by
picking out some of the feelings and emotions that most frequently
arise following the diagnosis of a child's handicap. Although
most parents will readily confirm that at some time or other
they experience most of the emotions I have listed, there are at
least three reasons why we should treat such a list with caution.

The first reason I have already given above. I pointed out
that the meaning of an event to an individual is more important
than the event itself when it comes to understanding that
individual's reaction. We cannot assume, therefore, that every
one of the emotional responses I listed will be aroused in every
mother and father of a handicapped child. What is important
for one will not be so important for the next.

Secondly, the experience of emotion is not always as simple
and clear-cut as a list of this sort may suggest. Emotions are
frequently blurred and confused, they vary in strength from one
person to the next and from one day to another. Furthermore,
people rarely stop to consider exactly what emotion they are
feeling at any given time, especially when they are in the middle
of a crisis. It is in fact quite possible to go through extremes
of emotion without ever being able to say what it is one has felt.

This takes us to the third reason why a simple list of
emotional responses is an inadequate way of viewing the parent's
reaction. Far from being a series of separate mental states
flowing through the mind in linear sequence, these emotions are
part and parcel of the parent's struggle actively to reorganize
their lives. Crises must be resolved in some way or another.
Feelings of fear and shame and guilt are powerful forces which
serve to impel the parents towards their own particular solutions.
We should therefore view these emotional responses in terms
of the parts they play in the wider processes of adjustment,
rather than viewing them as separate and self-governing entities.

Needless to say, it is impossible for us to predict in what
way a parent will readjust after the birth of a handicapped child;
there are simply too many variables at play, not the least of

which is the individual's own determination to overcome his problems. But what we can attempt to do is come to an understanding of the main dimensions along which readjustment takes place.

In the next chapter, I will look at readjustment in terms of the strain on the relation between husband and wife and on the life of the family as a whole, but first I would like to draw attention to what is probably the most important dimension in a parent's adjustment to the handicapped child itself.

Rejection, overprotection

A number of questions arise for parents who find themselves in the situation I have described. Should they, for example, accept the personal sacrifices that are involved in reorganizing their lives around the handicapped child, or should they try to keep things as they were and let the handicapped child fit in as best he can? Can they live with their negative feelings, or should they try to hide these away? Should they fulfil their parental obligations and look after their child at home, or should they send him away into permanent residential care?

It should already be clear that these parents are faced with the arousal and opposition of two incompatible sets of desires. On the one hand is the desire to nurse and protect the handicapped child, because it is their own. On the other hand is the desire to reject it, because it is deformed. Strong maternal and paternal drives, which cannot easily be crushed, are therefore set against more negative feelings such as resentment and the fear that one will not be able to cope. A balance must somehow be found between the two conflicting desires.

It has often been observed by those working in this field that the balance of forces can be weighted in either direction, but that the outcome of this conflict is frequently extreme. Many parents react strongly in one direction and spare no effort to have their child placed in an institution as soon as they can, or else direct a great deal of aggression towards him in the home. Others react in the opposite way and become utterly devoted to the needs of the child, often to such an extent that both child and family suffer. It is important to realize that these reactions are in fact two poles of a single 'dimension' along which readjustment takes place. At one end of the scale is overprotection, at the other end is outright rejection of the handicapped child.

44

· Parental reactions to the birth of a handicapped child

This dimension, Overprotection $><$ Rejection, is important to the parent of any child, regardless of its physical condition. Flugel refers to it when he says, in his study of the normal family, that:

'To some extent the individual inevitably sacrifices himself in becoming a parent; and this sacrifice of personal comforts, pleasures, satisfactions and ambitions does not as a rule take place without some degree of resentment being felt against those whose existence necessitates the sacrifice......though the existence of a strong counter-impulse towards maternal love will often ensure repression of those feelings into the unconscious.....'

Most mothers and fathers, as Flugel suggests, strike a happy balance between gain and loss, reward and disappointment following the birth of their child. It is not hard to see why this balance is so drastically upset when the child in question is deformed. Guilt and the fear of the strength of one's own hostile emotions tend to push parents into an overprotective attitude, whereas shame, resentment and horror urge them to reject the child. So strong are the forces involved that the scale tends to swing uncontrollably either one way or the other, rather than resting in equilibrium as it normally would.

It is enough at this stage to point out that whichever way this balance swings there are inevitable repercussions for the sibling. This, of course, is also true for the other reactions I have described. Just what these repercussions are will form the subject of later chapters in the book.

CONCLUSION

In this chapter I have tried to show that the birth of a handicapped child marks a crisis in the lives of its individual parents. I have suggested that in order to understand the meaning of this crisis to the individual parent, we should begin by exploring the expectations they held prior to the birth and diagnosis of their child. I then went on to examine some of the commonest features of the crisis on the level of simple emotional arousal, and finally pointed out certain preconditions to understanding the readjustments that a handicapped child demands of its parents. It merely remains to be said that I have not tried to lay down a rigid account of parental reactions in the hope that it may be applied to any and every parent of a handicapped child. To do so would be futile. Instead I have drawn upon my own observations and experience, and that of many others who work with the families of the handicapped, and who encounter the reactions I have described every day of their lives. What I have written in this chapter, and also in the next, is intended to be no more than a guideline to the sort of things that appear to happen in most of these families. For only when we have such a picture clearly in mind can we fully appreciate the problems with which siblings themselves are faced.

References

Ackerman, Nathan. 'The Psychodynamics of Family Life'. Basic Books, New York, 1958.

Caldwell, B. and Guze, S. A study of adjustment of parents and siblings of institutionalized and non-institutionalized retarded children. 'Amer. J. of Mental Def.', vol. 64, 1960.

Caplan, G. (Ed.), 'Prevention of Mental Disorders in Children'. Tavistock Publications, 1961.

Caplan, G. 'An Approach to Community Mental Health'. Tavistock Publications, 1961.

Carnegie UK Trust. 'Handicapped Children and their Families'. Dunfermline, Scotland, 1964.

Flugel, J.C. 'The Psychoanalytic Study of the Family'. Hogarth Press, London, 1921.

Goldie, L. Psychiatry of the handicapped family. 'Developmental Medicine and Child Neurology', vol. 8, no. 4, 1966.

Gould, B. Working with Handicapped Families. 'Case Conference', vol. 15, no. 5, 1968.

Hewett, S. 'The Family and the Handicapped Child'. Allen and Unwin, London, 1970.

Katz, A. 'Parents of the Handicapped'. Springfield, Ill., 1961.

Laing, R.D. 'The Politics of the Family'. CBC Publications, Toronto, 1969.

· Parental reactions to the birth of a handicapped child

Levinson, A. 'The Mentally Retarded Child'. Allen and Unwin, London, 1967.

Lomas, P. (Ed.) 'The Predicament of the Family'. Hogarth Press, London, 1967.

Mandelbaum, A. Groups for parents of retarded children. 'Children', vol. 14 no. 6, 1967.

Menolascino, F.J. Parents of the mentally retarded. 'J. of Amer. Acad. of Child Psychiatry' vol. 7, p. 589, 1968.

Olshansky, S. Chronic sorrow: a response to having a mentally defective child. 'Soc. Casework' vol. XLIII, no. 4, April, 1962.

Parfit, J. 'Spotlight on Groupwork with Parents in Special Circumstances'. National Children's Bureau, London, 1971.

Plutchik, R. 'The Emotions: Facts, Theories and a New Perspective'. Ramdom House, New York, 1962.

Prechtl, H.F.R. The mother-child interaction in babies with minimal brain damage. In 'Determinants of Infant Behaviour'. vol. II, Brian Foss (Ed.). Methuen, London, 1963.

Szasz, T. The communication of distress between child and parent. 'Br. J. of Med. Psychol.' vol. 32, 1959.

Winnicot, D.W. 'The Child and the Outside World'. Tavistock Publications, 1957.

5 Crisis in the family

'The impact of the arrival of a handicapped child on the life of a family is tremendous, sometimes overwhelming'

from 'Living with Handicap' — Younghusband et al.

In the last chapter I described the arrival of a handicapped child in terms of the more immediate effects it is likely to have on individual parents. I treated it, in other words, as a personal crisis for parents. In this chapter, I shall look at handicap not in terms of its effect on any one individual, but as the precipitator of a crisis in the family as a whole.

It would, of course, be wrong to suggest that there are two separate and independent crises taking place within the context of the event I am describing. The individual reactions of a mother and a father on hearing that their baby is handicapped represent family events as well as purely personal ones - what has changed when we view them as one rather than the other is our perspective on the event, not the event itself. In fact this chapter merely represents a second perceptual cut across the complex synthesis of a social phenomenon. It is an attempt to draw a graph in words of some of the forces at work upon that small unit of people held together by reciprocal needs and dependencies known as the family, at a time when one of their members is handicapped.

1. FAMILIES IN CRISIS

Once again it is necessary to begin on a note of caution. The graph I am drawing is of necessity general, built up as it were of average values over a wide range of readings. The particular families I am attempting to describe, however, are never in this sense average, and this is a point which cannot be over-stressed. Most of my remarks, for instance, will refer to nuclear families comprising two parents and at least two children. The pattern of relationships, and thus the collective experience of this sort of unit, will differ markedly from the family in which there is, say, an unmarried mother living with her children, or a widower living with his parents in law and his children, or, unlikely in this country but not unknown, a polygamous family.

Even for more average nuclear families, if they are subjected to a roughly similar 'event' there will still be a great diversity in their experience of that event, depending on a wide range of variables such as their size, the sex and age of their members, their social and economic situation, and so on. Furthermore, even families which are identical in all these demographic respects are likely to differ in terms of their internal organization. Experts have differentiated many sorts of family from the point of view of their social functioning, and distinctions such as the integrative as opposed to the centrifugal family (Jordan 1972) abound in the literature.

The family, then, although it is universal as a social unit in one form or another, consists in a great variety of groups which vary in structure as well as in purposive orientation. Because handicap cuts across all social strata, we are dealing here with an unselected cross-section of all these different sorts.

This means that it is very hard to make general statements about families with a handicapped child so that they will apply to any one particular family. The task is even harder when we take into consideration the range of physical and mental conditions which the all-inclusive label 'handicap' covers, and also the variety of circumstances in which handicaps are incurred and their diagnoses made.

Despite all these problems there is, I believe, a very real value in a general description of the crisis that handicap constitutes for a family, the only proviso to this being that we do not confuse description with definition. One cannot expect to fit every handicapped family into the general pattern I shall try to trace here, nor would there be any point in looking for precise statistical analysis of a discrete class of people in this chapter. Rather is it intended as an aid to our understanding, and it is with this in mind that I shall be examining some of the most salient problems and stresses that unquestionably do pertain to a wide range of families in which there is a handicapped child. Whether or not the general pattern is appropriate and useful to an understanding of any particular case is a matter of insight and judgement and can only be decided by the reader.

2. THE CONCEPT OF CRISIS IN THE FAMILY

In the last chapter, I referred to Caplan's concept of crisis. He used this word to denote 'what happens when a person faces a difficulty ... in which his existing coping repertoire is insufficient and he therefore has no immediate way of handling the stress'. Such a concept proved useful in looking at the reaction of parents to the birth of a handicapped child, but in developing this concept Caplan was quite clearly thinking about an individual's crisis rather than crisis in a group; it is therefore necessary to re-examine his concept with a view to using it in the context of the family. There is another reason for re-examining it, too, for although in its present form it captures the idea of breakdown implicit in the event, there are other important elements of which it fails to take account.

The most significant of these is clearly explicit in the original Greek word krisis from which our own word is derived. The noun krisis means, quite literally, a decision. Just as in medical terms the crisis of a fever is the turning point, the point at which the outcome of the battle between life and death is decided, so in social and psychological terms a crisis is a turning point in some state of affairs, a tipping of the balance of forces in one direction or another. The balance may be restored to its former equilibrium or pushed to a point where the forces at work are so unequal that they can no longer exist in conjunction and therefore give way to an entirely new field of forces and a subsequent restoration of equilibrium. The crisis in either case is the turning point in the balance.

It would be wrong, then, to regard crisis exclusively in terms of a person 'having no way to handle his stress'. Quite simply, people always do handle their stress, however great it may be. They may handle it in a variety of ways, some of which we may choose to regard as pathological; they may use all the defences under the sun in an effort to sheild themselves from pain; but whatever their reaction is, the stress is in some way being 'dealt with'.

Crisis, then, is not simply an emotional overload resulting in a static breakdown. Even when a person responds to stress by totally withdrawing from the world of reality, his very failure to act and respond is in itself a form of action, a form of response. It is one way of dealing with his stress.

In focusing on the idea of failure to cope in a crisis there is a danger of missing this essential element of any crisis; that it represents a turning-point, a moment of decision in the life of the person or indeed of the group. It is in fact this element of dis-equilibrium and subsequent reorganization that I would stress in using the concept to refer to family events.

What I would suggest is that the equilibrium of the family is generally upset by the arrival and presence of a handicapped child. Both the internal functioning of the family and the relations of the family with its outer environment are normally held in balance. In other words families normally have an adaptive capacity to remain relatively stable in the face of continuously changing demands and pressures. In the crisis that so often attends handicap, the stability of this balance is upset both in terms of the inner dynamics of the family life and in terms of the family's relations with the outside world.

Let us examine this concept of family crisis, then, against specific aspects of life in a family with a handicapped child.

3.   THE EFFECT ON BASIC FAMILY FUNCTIONS

It is generally agreed that from a sociological point of view the family fulfils four major functions for its respective members. These are: the socially approved provision of sex, the setting for reproduction, a self-sufficient economic unit and a mode of rearing and socializing children. Even before we look at the more intimate aspects of family life and dynamics, we can see that each one of these major functions can be radically affected by the presence of a handicapped child.

Sex

I have already drawn attention to the way in which handicap plays upon parental fears and fantasies about sex. Commonly, men feel that the birth of a handicapped child places a question-mark over their virility, especially if this is their first child. Women often feel that they are somehow 'bad inside'. With these sorts of feelings aroused, it is not hard for the sexual relationship of the parents to deteriorate. There may be mutual recriminations of impotence and a great deal of projection of feelings of guilt and failure on to the other partner. Often recriminations of this sort will be implied rather than openly asserted, which serves only to add to confusion and heighten estrangement within the relationship. The father may make desperate attempts to reassert his virility and 'prove himself', perhaps against the wishes of the mother who herself may live in fear of displeasing her husband, and even more in fear of the possibility of further conception. The intense and often ambivalent emotions that are aroused during the act of intercourse may well be felt by parents, if only in a half-conscious way, to lie at the very root of their baby's deformity.

Reproduction

It has been firmly established by Holt and also by Tizard and Grad that families with a retarded child more often than not decide to restrict the growth of their family. In Holt's study, out of 160 mothers who theoretically could have had more children, 101 decided not to. The decisions of 90 of these families appeared to be directly related to the presence of a retarded child. Lindy Burton (1972) also reported that 46 per cent of mothers of children with cystic fibrosis were afraid of getting pregnant and bearing another disabled child.

The family as an economic unit

The family as an economic unit is affected by handicap much more than has generally been appreciated. I have drawn attention elsewhere (1973) to the very considerable costs incurred by a handicapped child. In particular there are the expenses incurred by travelling to and from hospitals on a regular basis, taxi-fares for the transportation of children who cannot travel on public transport, the installation of telephones where these are necessary on medical grounds, moving to a house or flat which has ground floor access without steps, buying special clothes for the handicapped child and making adaptations in the home. In addition to such things, the family's income from employment is often threatened. Mothers frequently need to give up their employment altogether to attend to the special needs of their handicapped children. Meyerowitz and Kaplan, for example, found that mothers of children with cystic fibrosis often ceased their outside employment, and Hall, who made a study of families with cerebral palsied children, found that mothers of the more severely handi-

capped group were more likely to remain in the home than to take
outside employment. The problem does not only affect mothers;
Schonell and Watts found that 26 per cent of the fathers they
interviewed found it necessary to alter their career in some way
on account of their handicapped child.

For wealthy families the costs I have listed may seem slight,
but for many they represent a considerable disruption in the
economics of everyday life.

Child-rearing and socialization

Needless to say, the way in which normal child-rearing practice
is affected by the presence of a handicapped child forms the
subject of this book; it therefore requires only a cursory mention
here. As we shall see in subsequent chapters, child-rearing
practice in relation to able-bodied siblings is susceptible to many
adverse pressures when the parents in question are preoccupied
with a handicapped child. What I have not dealt with at any length
in this study, except insofar as it arises in connection with
siblings, is the nature of the parents' relationship with their
handicapped child. It is worth pointing out in the present context
that this, too, is likely to represent a considerable deviation
from the parents' expectations of child-rearing roles, or for that
matter from their already established patterns of child care.
The fact that there are on the market literally scores of books
and pamphlets on the subject of how to bring up a handicapped
child underlines the fact that handicapped children are not quite
normal subjects when it comes to child-rearing. Quite apart
from qualitative differences in approach, the rearing of a handicapped child requires above all a great deal of time - indeed one
modern trend, that has attracted a significant following in the
Western world, advocates the principle of maximizing stimulation
to children suffering from spasticity, paralysis or brain damage.
Parents are encouraged to spend not less than eight or ten hours
every day stimulating the muscles and minds of these children in
an effort to force them into activity. Those who resort out of
hope and desperation to extreme approaches of this sort must
totally reorganize both their own lives and those of their families
in order to 'bring-up' their handicapped child. One wonders,
incidentally, how often they weigh up their possible degree of
success against the likely detriment to family life.

So much for the four main sociological functions of the family.

We have seen that each one of them is threatened by disruption
if not actual termination as a result of the physical and emotional
aftermath of handicap. One could say without exaggeration that
the very foundations of the family as a social unit are threatened.

This does not mean that a family will necessarily fall apart
at the seams as soon as a handicapped child is born. As I have
suggested, families have an adaptive capacity to weather such
storms, and in fact there can be no doubt that some families
emerge from them stronger than they were before. But for all
that, handicap is a storm, and one moreover which does act as
a potential threat to the most basic structures of family life.
Pringle and Fiddes in the conclusion to their study of thalidomide
children make the following apt comment:

> 'The evidence suggests that the presence of a very severely
> disabled child in a family produces one of two diametrically
> opposed and extreme situations; either the parents cope
> admirably, indeed heroically, and the child thrives almost as
> well as any normal one; or the family proves unequal to the
> tremendous strain, the mother breaks down, the marriage
> flounders, and the child is either wholly rejected or causes a
> tension and dissent which is inevitably reflected in his own
> maladjustment'.

This conclusion is clearly consistent with a concept of family
crisis as disequilibrium followed by reorganization. The reorganization may work either for or against the preservation of the
family unit, but if Pringle and Fiddes are correct it will in either
case be decisive.

The changes in family life that I have examined so far are in
effect no more than the 'raw materials' of crisis. They are
merely the weights which disrupt the balance in family equilibrium
We have yet to examine the mechanics of the balance itself. Let
us change our focus, therefore, from this somewhat one-dimen-
sional catalogue of 'disruptions' to an examination of the inter-
personal dynamics of crisis in the families I have described.

In the following three sections I shall lean heavily on the
language and insights of role theory. It is true that there are
many other ways of structuring our perception of family crisis,
but there are probably few better ones. The theory of roles is
essentially an inter-personal theory and is therefore ideal for
application to inter-personal and inter-group processes, such as.
we are dealing with here. The concepts involved have crept into

everyday usage, yet they are still incisive enough to enable us to
understand the simple essence of quite complex social events.

4. CRISIS IN THE ROLE RELATIONSHIPS OF PARENTS

Families are held together by and large because they satisfy the
individual needs of their members. The way in which they are
held together may be usefully described as a series of interlocking role relationships. The concept of role is now well-
established in both sociological and casework theory, and perhaps
for this reason is used in many different ways. However, as
Timms has pointed out, there are two basic elements in all the
various notions of role: reciprocity and patterning. Of the
former he says:

> 'Reciprocity is involved in the very notion of role, since the
> role of father makes no sense without that of the child. The
> behaviour which makes a consistent whole and which we
> describe as the role of father gains its meaning and consistency
> by reference to the role of another, the child'.

The role played by one person towards another thus satisfies not
only the needs of the first person but also complements the role
played by the other. In this sense the role relationship is interlocking.

The element of patterning referred to by Timms is responsible for the 'consistency' of the role, or in other words for the
fact that in any given situation we know what action the role
demands of us. Very often this consistency takes its shape
according to our social expectations of how the role in question
should be played. In other words it is patterned on our perception
of social norms. The particular roles that exist in any given
family will depend on a number of things: the personality of the
individual member and the expectations he has of different roles;
the demands made by the other person in a role and the developing
cycle of family life which requires the family to occupy itself
with a progression of new tasks involving new role relationships.

Our understanding of all this is important to our understanding of a family crisis. Role theory provides a valuable theoretical
framework in which we can view the disequilibrium of family
affairs. What happens in a crisis is, quite simply, the breakdown of role-complementarity between family members. In
other words there is an upsetting of the balance which normally

exists between members by virtue of the reciprocal nature of the
roles they play.

Let me bring these abstract formulations back to the world
of concrete illustration, and relate them more specifically to
families with a handicapped child.

Case illustration 1

Mr Wilkins was a quiet, rather submissive man. At the age
of twenty he left a home in which his mother had indulged his
every need, to marry a girl who promised (though not of course
in words) to do very much the same. The girl for her part had
a strong need to 'mother' her husband. The marriage worked
well for a year or two. The roles performed by each partner
vis a vis the other were complementary: one wanting to
mother, the other wanting to be mothered. At about this time,
however, the girl gave birth to a child who had a serious
congenital deformity; it required a great deal of looking after.
Although on one level this child's condition came as a tremendous shock to both parents, on another level the mother not
only readjusted to the idea fairly quickly, but actually discovered a very real satisfaction from attending successfully to
the needs of the child, which were after all so much greater
than the needs of an ordinary child. The father, however, grew
increasingly unhappy and wanted the child to go into permanent
residential care so that they could 'get on with their life as
normal'. The mother began to get angry with her husband for
always moping about the house and grumbling while she was
martyring herself for the sake of the child. She exhorted him
to go out and do something useful for a change. In fact he
began spending more time visiting his parents, and at one
point looked as if he might return there at least temporarily
to live.

Without looking any further into the details of this case we can
see that the arrival of the handicapped child initiated a crisis in
this family. Whereas when they first got married their respective
roles complemented each other satisfactorily, as soon as the
handicapped child arrived, this balance in interlocking roles was
radically upset. The father no longer fulfilled the role of a
'helpless child' in the family because the mother now had a real
helpless child who provided a more satisfying fulfilment of her
need to be the all-powerful but martyred mother-figure. As far

as the husband was concerned, his role expectations were no
longer being met and he had passed into a state of depression on
this account and made very real attempts to regress to his life
as a child. For the wife it was almost as if a new contract of
marriage had been written. She no longer saw herself as tied to
her husband by the same role-relationship; instead she began to
look to him for something else, 'something useful for a change'.

Case illustration 2

Jane Humphreys was nine months old, had a very severe
bilateral cleft palate and was almost impossible to feed. Mrs
Humphreys, in turn, was almost completely preoccupied with
Jane. She had little time to attend to her other daughter,
Sarah, and at the end of the day was usually so exhausted that
she inevitably lost her temper with her husband. According to
Mrs Humphreys he had no conception of the problem she had
to cope with, and came home from work each day expecting
his meal to be ready as usual. He too got angry, however,
both with his wife and with Sarah who began to demand his
attention in the evenings much more than she had done before.
He said he didn't mind spending time with the children but he
couldn't stand Sarah romping all over him when he was
watching a programme on the television or reading the paper.
It later transpired that at about this time Mr Humphreys had
started an affair with another woman.
In this case, as in the last one, although the details presented
are far from complete, it can be clearly seen that the handicap
brought about considerable role-reorganization in the family. The
mother's role as 'mother' was intensified towards the handicapped
child but weakened towards the sibling, Sarah. Being unable to
find the fulfilment of her own needs in her mother, Sarah began
to look more to her father for the fulfilment of these needs. Mr
Humphreys, for his part, was unable to understand, or else
unable to accept that his wife's role had in fact undergone a
substantial change. Far less was he willing to change his own
role by acting as 'mother' to Sarah.
The final, and possibly most destructive, reorganization of
role relationships in this family concerned the marital pair.
Mrs Humphreys, being emotionally as well as physically over-
occupied with Jane, began to neglect her role as wife and this,
as far as Mr Humphreys was concerned, was all he needed to

push him into the arms of another woman (another 'wife') who, as it happened, had been waiting in the wings for just such an opportunity.

These two illustrations by no means exhaust the possibilities of role reorganization in families with a handicapped child. The balance of a family's role-relationships can be upset in many different ways. Parents may disagree, for example, about what role the child should play in the family or about what role they themselves should play towards it. Those who saw the play or the film version of 'A day in the death of Joe Egg', which was based, I believe, on the author's personal experience, will appreciate the destructive effects of such role discrepancies on a marital relationship.

Some parents may be unfamiliar with the roles required of them, having no experiences on which to 'pattern' their responses or they may have failed to identify the particular roles that are required; alternatively they may have insufficient resources for playing a required role, or simply be unwilling to do so. Others who are particularly identified with their professional and social roles frequently feel that these are incompatible with their newly acquired role of mother and nurse to a permanently dependent child. In such cases the crisis can only be resolved by radically modifying, or perhaps even abandoning, one or other of these roles. Many women in this situation will look for a solution by placing their child in residential care, although others will abandon their outside commitments and turn their energies inwards in an affirmation of their family roles. Such parents make a conscious decision to adjust as an integrated family unit to any problem they may meet. In either case, however, the crisis of handicap marks a clearly defined turning point in family life.

For families who are weighed under with multiple problems before the birth of a handicapped child, the crisis of handicap is far less easy to distinguish in terms of role change than the examples I have already cited. Here, handicap is merely one extra problem to rest its weight upon the already sagging structures of the family. Quite a large number of multiple-problem families are visted by ICAA social workers, and for many of these it is impossible to assess realistically the effect of handicap on the dynamics of family life.

What for most families is a tragic event, an assault against expectations and a precedent for qualitative changes in family

organization, is often for these families no more than an
additional burden of care. More often than not they expect disappointment to attend whatever they do; they expect things to go
wrong. Sometimes, it is true, handicap is the last straw, the
final blow which pushes the family over the threshold of collapse.
But even so, collapse is hard to define, for these families may
have repeated reconciliations after what would otherwise have
appeared to be final separations.

Most parents, then, need to reassess their marital relationship in the light of their experience of handicap. They will need
to explore their individual feelings and reactions, perhaps
especially those secret feelings that I looked at in the last
chapter. They will need to assess the changes that have been
wrought in the roles they are playing within the family, and
somehow they must reorganize their new roles in a way that
is mutually satisfying. Where families fail to reach a mutual
agreement on these matters, or, worse, when they fail to discuss
them at all, there is every chance that they will in some way or
another disintegrate as a unified group and live in conflict, disharmony or actual separation.

5.   ARREST IN THE FAMILY LIFE-CYCLE

So far I have been looking mainly at the crisis in role comple-
mentarity for parents of a handicapped child. But role reorganizations also take place within the family on two others levels:
1. in terms of the relationships between children and their
siblings and 2. in terms of the relationships between parents
and children. I shall be looking in some detail at the relationships between children and siblings, with particular reference
to sibling rivalry, in a later chapter. Here I would like to concentrate briefly on one particular aspect of the relationship
between parents and children.

It was Bernard Farber who first drew attention to what he
called the revision of age and sex roles in families with a mentally retarded child. His argument went roughly as follows:
that all parents normally assign a status to each child in terms
of what they believe he is capable of doing. Normally this status,
and the roles and expectations it embodies, will develop as the
child grows older. In other words, what the parents regard as
the mental age of the child will roughly correspond to his
chronological age. Farber points out that age-grading in a

culture is regarded as more of a psychological and social activity than a purely chronological variable, for example a severely retarded individual who is in fact over the age of twenty-one is still generally regarded as a child by those with whom he interacts. As if in formal recognition of this, the Hutterite religious group excludes the mentally retarded from adult responsibility by cancelling baptism requirements, thereby giving them the moral status of children.

This constant redefinition of the social and mental ages of the child is a very important aspect of family dynamics according to Farber, for not only do a child's roles change along with his changing status within the family, but this very fact means that the parents are continually being prompted to redefine their own roles, obligations and values in accordance with the changing roles of the child.

This means that the process of children being born, growing up and eventually leaving home, constitutes a cycle in the life of a family. At the end of the cycle the parents' roles towards their grown-up children are quite different from what they were in the early stages when the children were young.

Farber maintains that in families with a severely retarded child, the life-cycle of the family is interrupted, and sometimes completely arrested. Because the retarded child may never 'grow up' the parent's role towards him remains constant, whereas towards an ordinary child it would develop and change. The parents are in fact bound up in roles which are appropriate to one stage in the family's life-cycle. They may be prevented from ever reaching the later stages because the cycle itself has been arrested.

In terms of the other children in the family, although the retarded child may be the oldest in a chronological sense, he quickly becomes the youngest both mentally and socially. This means that children who would normally have remained, say two or three years younger or older than their sibling, will in these families constantly need to revise their age and sex roles vis a vis the retarded child.

In what sense does this arrest in the family's life-cycle constitute a crisis? Farber's research would suggest that, if anything, it affects the siblings more than the parents. He found that the relationship of siblings to their mothers was adversely affected and he relates this in particular to the degree of dependency of the retarded child. The more of a 'child' the retarded

person was, in other words, the more the sibling's relationship
with his mother tended to suffer.

Another significant factor appeared to be the degree to which
siblings had to revise their birth-order roles vis a vis the
retarded child. Graliker, Fishler and Koch found, for example,
that when there was a ten-or-more year age-gap between retarded
children and their siblings (siblings being the older) there was
less likely to be an adverse effect on the siblings. Farber's
conclusion from this was:

> 'These findings suggest that when the normal siblings are much
> older than the retarded child, there is little need to modify the
> birth-order roles in the family. Without this revision of roles,
> apparently, the normal siblings are not profoundly affected by
> the presence of the retarded child. '

Clearly, however, the absence of role-revision is not the only
element that would be responsible for the relative health and
stability of these older siblings.

It is important to stress that Farber's work was related only
to families in which there was a retarded child and therefore none
of his conclusions apply to families where the handicapped child
is merely physically disabled. Nevertheless it is true to say
that the physically disabled child often remains at a stage of
childish dependence on a practical level, even though he may be
fully mature in an intellectual sense. Therefore there may still
be some element of arrest in the family's development along the
lines that Farber suggests.

6. CHANGE IN RELATIONS BETWEEN THE FAMILY AND THE COMMUNITY

One aspect of the crisis following this arrest affects families of
both mentally and physically handicapped children, namely the
revision demanded in their relations with the wider community.
In constrast to some other areas of handicap, quite a lot of
research has been conducted into the restriction of family par-
ticipation in extra-family relationships. On the whole the research
points out exactly what one would expect, that because of the
exceptional care-problems associated with many handicapped
children, (and indeed for older handicapped persons who remain
'children'), parents are often tied to their homes; this tends to
isolate them from friends and sometimes leads to deep feelings

of loneliness. Isolation of this sort can easily be exacerbated by
the shame that some parents feel whenever they 'display' their
handicapped child in public, although most parents seem to overcome these feelings. Perhaps even more significant in this
respect is the avoidance-response of the public at large when
faced with handicapped people. Irving Goffman, amongst others,
has drawn attention to the unease which able-bodied people
generally feel in the presence of the handicapped, especially when
they are not personally familiar with handicapped people and their
problems.

A combination of these factors is undoubtedly responsible
for research findings such as those of Holt, who reported that
40 per cent of the parents he interviewed were unable to go out
together and a smaller percentage were unable to take a vacation.
Similarly Tizard and Grad found that 45 per cent of families with
a mentally retarded child living at home had limited social contacts. They also found that these families had a lower material
standard of living and considerably more management problems
than families without a handicapped child. Schonell and Watts,
in their Australian study, found that 50 per cent of families
reported that handicap had an adverse effect on their capacity to
visit other homes, and 22 per cent that it had an adverse effect
on the selection of people to visit their own home.

The only piece of research to disagree with this general
trend of findings was that of Sheila Hewett. Throughout her
report she stressed that families with a handicapped child seemed
to be able to cope as well as any other sort of family. On the
subject of isolation she concluded that:

'It seemed that feelings of isolation were much more a function
of the mother's personality than of the presence of a handicapped child. '

She conceded, however, that:

'The plight of mothers who are lonely and who do feel cut off,
is very real. '

and she points out that this is more likely to happen in rural
areas where problems of transport and finding friends in a
similar situation can be very great. Hewett does quote one
mother, moreover, who lived in an urban area and who did have
friends and family around her but who, despite these things,
answered in the following way when asked if she felt lonely or

isolated:

> 'Yes I do in some ways because you're so busy looking after
> them that you haven't got time for going out.... As I say,
> with her feeding she was very, very slow. Well, by the time
> she'd finished her feeding and that and I'd tidied round, it'd
> be time for her sister coming in at dinner-time - well, it was
> an effort to get out. I used to make myself go out on a Friday,
> to take her out in the pram and that. But I wouldn't like to go
> through it again, definitely not. I mean it probably sounds a
> little bit selfish, saying you get no outside entertainment, but
> I think you need it, and as I say, being on your own, you feel
> that nobody else has got this problem and you've got nobody to
> talk to about it. I mean you tell your friends and that, and
> they pop in and see you but they don't understand the same -
> they say they do - they say "Oh she'll be alright", but I mean,
> even so, you've still got that loneliness.'

One interesting piece of research data was obtained by Meyerowitz and Kaplan who showed that when parents did go out socially
to any great extent without their handicapped child, they tended
to display more somatic symptoms of stress (such as ulcers)
than parents who stayed at home. Farber maintains that this is
consistent with his own research findings on families with
severely retarded children where 'women faced with role-organ-
ization crisis often developed physical symptoms'.

There can be no doubt on the whole, then, that the family's
relationship to the wider community undergoes considerable
stress and change. For families who are socially aspiring, this
can result in an unbearable situation. The entire purposive
organization of the family, to 'get on' and 'do well' in the social
and economic struggles of life, may seem to be jeopardized by
the impact of handicap upon them.

It is not surprising, in view of this, that the act of labelling
the handicapped child assumes a great importance to many
parents. The label they use to describe the child, whether
'brain injured' or 'spastic' or 'a bit backward' or 'mentally
retarded', for example, will depend on the way they wish to present him to the outside world. And since that world is so prone
to misunderstand and pre-judge the meaning of labels, it is, if
anything, surprising that even more parents don't go for 'a little
bit backward' rather than terms like 'mentally retarded'. 'We
live on a council estate', said the mother of a child with spina-

bifida. 'Some people think his condition is catching and others say how wonderful to have a special child. I say nothing but I cry inside.'

7. SUMMARY AND CONCLUSION

In this chapter I began by suggesting that handicap marks a crisis in the life of a family and I pointed out that every area of family functioning was vulnerable to this crisis. I then attempted to explore the dynamics of crisis in terms of the sudden and often devastating role reorganizations that take place both inside the family and in its social relations with the community at large.

I have tried throughout to stress that families vary in the degree to which they are affected by handicap and in the degree to which they are able to cope with crisis. The birth of a handicapped child is, after all, a variable which intervenes in an already highly complex and unique situation. The state of the marriage, the openness of parents with one another and their children, their expectations of family achievement and of the roles of individual family members, their past experience of coping with crisis, their individual inadequacies, ... all of these factors, and many more besides, are brought to the surface when the family is confronted by the crisis of handicap, a crisis which will in addition demand solutions to many problems they have never before had to face.

With so many factors at work, this chapter is necessarily only a pointer to the plight of individual families. There will be many variations on the themes I have described. The unmarried mother is a case in point. She has the arguable advantage of not having to align her reactions to those of a spouse, which in some families is a major source of conflict and distress. On the other hand, of course, she lacks the emotional support a husband can give, and may be unable to find anyone who will share the unenviable addition to her domestic load.

There are many other variations such as this. Although the particular circumstances affecting each of them, and indeed the particular way in which any family crisis occurs, must be regarded as unique, there is nevertheless, as I have tried to show, a basic structure of family crisis in respect of handicap, a structure which cuts across the uniqueness in the texture of events.

In the report of the Carnegie UK Trust it was stressed that

· Crisis in the family

'there is a different kind of balance in the family containing a
handicapped child, a restructuring of attitudes which has implications for all members of the family'. I hope in this chapter
that I have provided some insight into the nature of that balance
and some of the ways in which these roles may be restructured.

References

Burton, L. An investigation into the problems occasioned for
   the child with cystic fibrosis. A paper given to the 84th
   AGM of the ICAA. London, November 1972.

Caplan, G. 'An Approach to Community Mental Health'.
   Tavistock Publications, London, 1961.

Caplan, G. Prevention of mental disorders in children. In
   'An Approach to Community Mental Health'. Tavistock
   Publications, London, 1961.

Carnegie UK Trust. 'Handicapped Children and their Families'.
   Dunfermline, Scotland, 1964

Farber, B. 'Mental Retardation: Its Social Context and Social
   Consequences'. Houghton and Mifflin, New York, 1968.

Goffman, E. 'Stigma'. Prentice Hall, New Jersey, 1963.

Graliker, B., Fishler, K. and Koch, R. Teenage reaction to
   a mentally retarded sibling. 'American Journal of Mental
   Def.' vol. 66, no. 8, 1962, p. 838.

Hewett, S. 'Handicapped Children and their Families'.
   University of Nottingham Press, 1970.

Holt, K. The influence of a retarded child upon family
   limitation. 'J. of Ment. Def. Res.', vol. 2, part 1, June
   1958.

Jordan, W. 'The Social Worker in Family Situations'.
   Routledge and Kegan Paul, 1972.

Kew, S. The cost of handicap. 'British Hospital Journal'.
   vol. LXXXIII, no. 4330, 1973.

National Bureau for Co-operation in Child Care. 'Living with
   Handicap'. London, 1971.

Nichols, P. 'A Day in the Death of Joe Egg'. Faber, London,
   1967.

Pringle, K. et al.   'The Challenge of Thalidomide'. Longman, London, 1970.

Schonell, F. and Watts, B. A first survey on the effects of a subnormal child on the family unit. 'Amer. J. of Ment. Def.' no. 61, 1957, p. 210.

Sifneos, P. A concept of emotional crisis. 'Mental Hygiene'. vol. 44, no. 2, 1960.

Timms, M. 'Social Casework: Principles and Practice'. Routledge, 1964.

Tizard, J. and Grad, J. 'The Mentally Handicapped and Their Families'. Oxford University Press, 1961.

6 Attention-seeking behaviour

'In matters of the body it is possible to make mistakes, even to allow rickets, and yet rear a child with nothing worse than bow-legs. But on the psychological side, a baby deprived of some quite ordinary but necessary thing such as affectionate contact, is bound to some extent to be disturbed in emotional develop-ment, and this will show in personal difficulty as the young child grows up.'

D. W. Winnicott.

Attention-seeking behaviour was the most commonly reported sign of disturbance amongst the siblings known to caseworkers. In some cases this behaviour was neither sufficient in degree nor severe enough in kind to be regarded as a real source of worry, in others it was held to be evidence of deep disturbance in the child. Children of all ages and from all backgrounds like to draw attention to themselves at times, and as a 'form' of childhood behaviour there is nothing necessarily unusual or disturbing about this. There comes a point, however, when the child's search for attention must be regarded as a sign of disturbance insofar as he is searching, primarily, not merely for attention but for help with a particular difficulty or conflict which he is unable to resolve on his own.

In the present chapter I shall point to various ways in which siblings were felt to be doing just this. I shall also point out how their behaviour might be regarded as both appropriate and in-appropriate given the situation with which they are faced, and finally I shall draw attention to some of the reactions which such behaviour elicits from the family itself.

CASE ILLUSTRATION 1. THE PORTER FAMILY

SK: The handicapped child here is very severely handicapped with a heart condition and brain damage.

MB: I think the two siblings here are both thoroughly 'normal' children, although the eldest of them I expect I've put down as 'mildly disturbed'.

SK: Yes, you have.

MB: This child at one time was extremely jealous of his handicapped brother and couldn't let the mother pick him up, touch him, or go near him without making a fuss, creating a scene. He was looked upon very much as a rival baby. The mother certainly gives a lot of attention to the eldest child and most of this is necessary because he is a very delicate and helpless child who needs everything doing for him, and I've seen the other boy hanging round his mother's skirt in a very pathetic way as if to say, 'won't anyone look at me and do something for me?'

SK: Is this something the mother sees as a problem?

MB: At the time I filled this out, the mother was too wrapped up in her other child to notice the sibling; she really couldn't focus any attention on the other child at all. She was very upset about the handicapped boy but more recently things have changed in the family. In fact, I saw the mother this morning; she came to the mothers' group with both children and the little one managed to go off and play with the other children without any qualms at all. He certainly seems much more secure now.

SK: Does he play with his handicapped brother at all?

MB: Not much. Almost whenever I've seen them in the past, the eldest one has been occupying the mother's attention and the three-year-old has been trying to interrupt and to get attention for himself. Whenever she picks up the handicapped one, his brother is there waiting to be picked up as well, and if she puts the handicapped child down, he's still there clamouring for his turn to be picked up. It's a very clear-cut situation. I don't think it's fair to say that it's the mother's fault here, there have been so many things wrong with the eldest child, the mother has naturally been extremely worried and upset and this has just thrown her completely out of balance with regard to the rest of the family. I think basically she's a good mother but she's been so wrapped up in the handicap that she just hasn't realized what's happened to the other child.

CASE ILLUSTRATION 2. THE GOODRIDGE FAMILY

WK: I regard this family as one which provides a striking example of the problems for siblings.

SK: What sort of problems have there been?

WK: Well, first of all, the parents find it very difficult to accept their physically handicapped sons. Both boys are suffering from a high degree of muscular dystrophy and both have been chair-bound from an early age. It was perhaps because they have never been able to come to terms properly with these handicaps that the parents literally made themselves martyrs in attending to the needs of these handicapped boys. They were offered help all along by the Health and Welfare Department, by all kinds of social workers, and for a long time, on many occasions, they refused all help. I feel that the brothers and sisters have suffered a great deal as a result of the parents' behaviour. The eldest girl seemed to have safeguarded her own existence by opting out of the family. She would have nothing to do with the family whatsoever; she isolated herself from them so much that although she was living in the same house, she even ate her meals in her own room and wouldn't come downstairs to the family meal, and, in fact, since then she has found a husband and has left the family and has no contact with them at all. The eighteen-year-old girl has had a lot of delinquent problems.

SK: What sort of problems?

WK: She has been caught stealing and spent a number of nights away from home at the age of about fifteen and, as a result of all this, she was installed in a special hostel for girls in London where she now works, and in fact as soon as she started living in this hostel and working from there, everything was all right and she only visited her family in the holidays.

SK: And what about the twelve-year-old?

WK: The twelve-year-old has had all sorts of difficulties and it's a very long story. First of all he was suffering from nocturnal enuresis and encopresis, both of which were very bad. This was always much worse during the holidays and in fact at school he was always all right. The school knew him as a very good boy doing his best, of average intelligence, nicely spoken and friendly.

SK: But in the home?

WK: In the home it was trouble all along, the mother always complained about doing his extra laundry.

SK: Do you think these were realistic complaints? Was this a problem that you literally saw, or do you think the mother was just making a fuss?

WK: No, I saw them; in fact, first of all he was attending for psychiatric treatment on the recommendation of the family doctor. The psychiatrist saw this boy on three occasions after which the appointments were dropped by the mother who, at this point, said that it was too far to go to see the psychiatrist every week. I followed this up as best I could and arranged for the child to see the child guidance clinic locally. In fact, he went and saw a psychiatrist there; it very quickly came out with this psychiatrist that the boy was very jealous of his two handicapped brothers. He said that Jonathan wanted to have the attention from his parents that they received; his mother used to change the muscular dystrophy boys and always helped them on the toilet, yet didn't do this with Jonathan. The psychiatrist diagnosed this as lying at the root of his soiling problem and after a course of treatment with him, this problem stopped.

SK: Did the mother also help to solve this problem by spending more time with the boy, and looking after his needs more closely?

WK: She did, yes, but the problems in this family were solved eventually when the two muscular dystrophy boys went into residential care.

SK: What made you feel, in this family, that it was the handicapped children who were causing all the upsets with these siblings, especially the elder two?

WK: The eldest girl especially used to talk about this a lot, she used to say she found it very aggravating when the parents carried the boys upstairs and downstairs all the time and pampered them and did all the things for them that they had to do. All the siblings here have been left very much in the background while the two handicapped ones have been the focus of the parents' attention for many many years.

• Attention-seeking behaviour

CASE ILLUSTRATION 3. THE SPURRELL FAMILY

JB: The one who is seriously disturbed here is Stephen.

SK: The second one, the eight-year-old?

JB: Yes. He steals; he used to do the most diabolical things,
like taking the electric kettle, filling it up with water and putting
it on the gas. He is not stupid but he will just do this. He'll
go and smash the windscreens of lorries and cars. He'll slash
tyres and then he'll go to the people and say 'your tyres have
been let down' and he'll perhaps get two bob from the people
for telling them this and then they'd realize the tyres have been
slashed and they can tell it's him.

SK: Is he aggressive in the home?

JB: Yes, he resents John, the handicapped twin, very much.
He says he hates him. I've never seen it but the mother says
he kicks him and throws things at him. What I've seen when I'm
there is that the mother has got John on her lap and Michael,
who is the third one, and Stephen are continually fighting for the
mother. They are doing things so that she has to give them
attention. John is sitting on her knees and Stephen is pestering
her, like pulling her hair, just little things like that, but all
the time.

SK: How does the mother react to all this? Does she always
try and stop them fighting and protect the handicapped one, or
is she partly behind them?

JB: No, she tries to protect John. She used to react in a very
damaging way with Stephen; she used to shout at him and scream
at him. We talked about it a lot and she sees it now in terms of
the lack of attention that Stephen feels he is getting - the same
with Michael - and now she tries to give a bit more time to
Stephen and Michael in order to remedy this, but it is an
incredibly difficult situation in the home. It's a small flat, he
can't go out anywhere, there's one small lounge; the handicapped
child is permanently in the middle of it. Michael can't do anything, because whatever he does, he is liable to injure John, so
he's always been sat upon by his mother - 'don't do this, you'll
hurt John, no you can't have this', etc. The mother is trying
to protect John all the time. She does her best: I think she's
bloody marvellous; the place is beautifully kept .... but what
chance have they really got?

I do not want to discuss the ways in which these three case-situations should be handled. To do this we would in any event need much more information than I have presented here.· My only purpose at present is to draw attention to the observed link between a sibling's loss of attention and his subsequent development of a particular sort of behaviour; behaviour which we would describe as 'attention-seeking'.

In these cases, Jeremy Porter, Jonathan Goodridge and Stephen Spurrell, respectively, were all perceived as engaging in attention-seeking behaviour in a relatively consistent way and for a relatively prolonged period of time. Jeremy Porter 'was extremely jealous of his handicapped brother and couldn't let the mother pick him up, touch him or go near him without making a fuss, creating a scene.' He was perceived as 'hanging round his mother's skirt in a very pathetic way as if to say, "won't anyone look at me and do something for me?"' And almost whenever the caseworker saw him he was 'trying to interrupt and get attention for himself.' Jonathan Goodridge was seen to be claiming the attention of his mother by persistently soiling and wetting. He was diagnosed by the psychiatrist who saw him as 'wanting the attention from his parents that his handicapped brothers received.' Stephen Spurrell, in the third family, indulged in rather more bizarre ways of drawing attention to himself: by stealing, putting the electric kettle on the gas ring, smashing car windows and slashing tyres. He, too, was perceived as 'continually fighting for the mother' and 'doing things so that she has to give him attention.'

These three cases were chosen from many others of a similar sort. Although the circumstances of each of these families and the experiences of each of the children may differ widely in many respects from one case to the next, they all have in common the predominance of this sort of attention-seeking behaviour on the part of one or more of the siblings.

THE PURPOSE OF ATTENTION-SEEKING BEHAVIOUR

What makes an intelligent child take an electric kettle, fill it up with water, and put it on a gas ring when he knows perfectly well what the consequence of this action will be? The answer, surely, is precisely because at some level of consciousness he does know what the consequence of the action will be, for not only will the underside of the kettle burn, but his mother will come in from the other room where she was feeding the handi-capped brother and make a fuss about what he has done. She may even tell his father about it when he comes home from work, which will make a change from their usual conversation about his chair-bound brother, John, and with a bit of luck he will be mentioned to the lady from the agency who also comes to talk about his chair-bound brother. All in all this little piece of adventure may not solve the problem of his own neglect (which made him embark on it in the first place), but it will at least reassure him that someone still cares, even if they care only enough to scold him.

In the cases cited above the children reacted in a variety of ways and in varying degrees. The mildness or severity of these reactions should not be allowed to obscure the fact that the under-lying structure of each response is essentially the same. It is the same insofar as all attention-seeking behaviour serves a particular purpose and is directed towards a specific develop-mental goal. Superficially this goal is the obvious one of gaining parental attention, but it is not attention as such which these children so desperately need, for although the origin and purpose of their behaviour will often remain unconscious to the children themselves, it is, in fact, a function of their thwarted need for affectionate contact and love; for what they are hoping to find is the reassurance that they are still being supported in a stable relationship of love.

PARENTAL NEGLECT OF SIBLINGS

It is not hard to see why so many siblings indulge in this sort of behaviour. As we have seen, most parents are thrown off balance by the discovery that their child is handicapped. The time and energy they spend on re-adjusting to this fact often means that there is a corresponding decrease in the time and energy they spend on siblings.

Childhood deprivation and neglect has received a great deal of attention in recent years and its consequences are generally well enough known to need only a cursory mention here. Much of the earlier work of Spitz, Levy, Anna Freud and Bowlby has been substantiated by numerous systematic studies, and their major conclusions about the effects of emotional deprivation are now beyond dispute, even though their methods and some of the values implicit in their work have come in for a lot of criticism recently.

Although there is little in these studies that is of immediate
relevance to us here, the general principle they extol of the
damaging effects of long-term parental neglect is one which is
obviously significant in terms of the families I am describing.

FACTORS CONDUCIVE TO THE NEGLECT OF SIBLINGS

Our society has in recent decades placed a high premium on the
value of motherhood. When we think of a mother neglecting her
children, therefore, we are likely to be filled with a sense of
outrage and feelings of reprehension. In the present context we
should remember, however, that the mothers and fathers of
handicapped children often cannot avoid becoming preoccupied
with these children to the possible detriment of their siblings.
Fortunately the 'normal' parental responses outlined in chapters
4 and 5 are part of a process of adjustment and therefore they do
not usually persist for very long periods of time, although sometimes, especially when they play upon personal and marital weaknesses, there is a danger of their becoming well-entrenched
patterns of behaviour.
    Neglect of siblings, of course, is not always just a question
of parents being preoccupied with their handicapped child for
emotional reasons of their own. There are frequently sound
medical and practical reasons why they must expend a great deal
of their energy in attending to the needs of such a child. Disability often involves some degree of functional impairment. The
children afflicted may not be able to climb stairs, go to the toilet,
dress, wash or eat without assistance from a parent. If they
want to go out it is often the parent who must take them; moreover, although disability does not necessarily imply illness,
disabled people often are ill or in need of an operation or simply
a hospital visit. Such needs impose a realistic practical obligatio
on parents. As a caseworker said of one child:

> 'Maria is so handicapped and you cannot neglect a severely
> handicapped child. She needs to be attended to constantly. She
> dribbles all the time and needs everything doing for her; the
> father is completely focused on her but then she needs his
> attention and he's got to give it to her otherwise she wouldn't
> exist; she just wouldn't survive.'

In a study of the families of polio victims, Davis observed the
same sort of indulgence of the handicapped child when he was

hospitalized, even though the child in question did not necessarily have any medical or physical need for the indulged and centralized position accorded to him within the family by the parents. Davis says (1963 p 163):

'Naturally the supreme object of the indulgence and concern of all family members, in particular the parents, was the hospitalized child himself. Since he was situated for the time being outside the family setting and removed from its customary disciplinary controls, the parents had almost no other recourse but to heap special indulgences upon the child; all other relational modes were, given the situation, effectively closed to them. For example, even among the poorest families in the study, it was common for parents to initiate elaborate programs of gift-giving (e.g. a new set of toys every week), frequently far beyond the child's capacity to utilize the gifts and the parent's ability to afford them. Similarly, many of the mothers would sneak in favourite foods to the child on visiting days, a practise explicitly forbidden by hospital regulations. These tangible indulgences of the sick child, not to mention the many intangible emotional ones bestowed upon him, were justified typically by the parents as attempts "to keep his spirits up so that he'll have the will to get well." '

This sort of over-indulgence was not confined to the child's period of hospitalization. Davis points out that:

'Much as they might have wished or thought it advisable to do so, the parents could not immediately upon the child's return abandon the many kindnesses and special indulgences that for months past they had lavished upon him.'

He found, moreover, that 'the difficulty of abandoning the parental policy of greater leniency and indulgence towards the children...' led to 'conflict, indecisiveness, and inconsistencies' within the families he studied.

In any case of severe handicap, then, we can trace at least two separate factors which are potentially conducive to the parental neglect of siblings. These arise respectively from the immediate practical needs of the handicapped child on the one hand, and the emotional needs of the parents on the other. As a result of these needs (it makes little difference whether we view them as being 'first-order' needs or 'second-order' needs) it was not uncommon for caseworkers to describe the handicapped child as lying at the physical as well as the emotional centre of the family. One family that falls into this group was described by its worker as follows:

> 'The youngest child, Jimmy, is severely mentally and physically handicapped. He really is a vegetable. He lies on the settee in the middle of the living room all the time. Everything has to be done for him, yet the parents are totally devoted to him and get very angry if the older children don't pay what is considered to be sufficient attention to Jimmy. If one of the children leaves the house without saying goodbye to Jimmy, Dad blows his top, whereas in fact it means nothing to Jimmy as he is incapable of understanding. The parents don't want the children to ignore him. Life is very much centred on Jimmy and meeting his needs.'

In this family, the father himself came from a somewhat deprived background and was described as wanting desperately to compensate for the paucity of his own childhood experience by creating a 'successful' family of his own. This was one of the reasons behind his total preoccupation with Jimmy; he was emotionally unable to accept the reality of Jimmy's condition because to do so would come too near to an intolerable admission of his own personal failure.

Clearly this combination of the realistic dependancy of the child and the emotional overconcern of its parents can create an unbearable situation for the other children in a family. Even if parents go out of their way to compensate these able-bodied children in other ways, it will be hard to forestall their feelings that they're not getting the attention they deserve.

As we have already seen, the sibling responds to his loss of attention by an increase in behaviour which is motivated by the desire to reclaim the attention he has lost, or at least to command that degree of attention and quality of affection to which, as a child, he has a right and feels a need.

The 'ploys' which children use to achieve this end differ widely, and although the primary task of the social worker must be to understand the structure of the child's experience and the motivational basis of his behaviour, it is clearly essential to look at some of the external forms which that behaviour may take. Let us look, therefore, at some of the various ploys that children used, according to caseworkers, in their attempts to gain attention in response to the situation just described.

SIBLINGS' REACTIONS

1. Disruptive behaviour

If a parent spends too much time and thought on his handicapped child, the sibling will want to distract his attention. Behaviour which disrupts the parents' normal interaction with the handicapped child is therefore extremely common. Disruptive behaviour of this sort is likely to appear whenever the parent shows signs of concern about the other child. The following description is typical of the reactions of many young children in this situation.

> 'She is very attention seeking. During all of my visits she tries by hook or by crook to attract her mother's attention and her usual way of reacting is just to become a screen between me and her mother when we are talking, she just gets in between us and whenever mother mentions Jacqueline's name, that's the handicapped girl, the younger girl comes out with some sort of special query or special demand and she frequently tries to distract the mother's attention altogether and won't let her talk about Jacqueline in her presence. All the things that Jacqueline wants the other one wants immediately to have the same. Of course I do know that in every family the younger child tends to be highly competitive and tends to race up the older one. I am sure this is a general trend, but with this little girl, it is magnified to the n'th degree.'

Disruptive behaviour, like many of the 'ploys' described here, serves two elementary functions for the sibling. It acts first of all as a mode of expression for his feeling of jealousy, and as such represents an attempt to communicate to the parent that a need is not being met. Secondly, it represents an attempt to control the behaviour of the parent by 'blotting out' the part of it that is the cause of so much pain.

2. Clinging

When the parent is out of sight or reach the sibling no longer has this control over the parents action and thought. He may therefore cling to his parents in a very literal sense in order not to lose the control that he wants. A number of cases of 'school phobia' and truanting were reported where this was clearly happening. Quite apart from the element of control in clinging, it is also an instinctive childhood response in moments of fear

77

and stress; through contact on a physical level the child can gain reassurance that he is safe and still loved.

3. Tantrums

Many children throw tantrums in order to attract attention to their frustrated demands, and this was no exception amongst the siblings in the sample. Once again screaming fits and tantrums are not only expressive from a personal point of view, but also are extremely pragmatic for the frustrated child. They help him in his efforts to steal the mother's attention away from the other child and redirect it onto himself.

4. Psychosomatic pains

If a handicapped child commands the attention of parents, what better method of winning attention for oneself than developing a handicap of one's own? One little boy whose unconscious logic had brought him to this conclusion developed the same 'symptoms' in his legs as his handicapped sister had in hers. The only difference between the two children was that one of them had very real gangrene in her only surviving leg, whereas the other had no apparent physical cause for his pain.

As the caseworker pointed out, there is an element of 'identification' in this particular ploy, which is undoubtedly present in many siblings in a less dramatic form. It is not unusual for a child to identify with another person whom he sees to be enjoying the very thing that he himself most wants.

5. Promiscuity

Promiscuity amongst older siblings was sometimes cited as evidence of sibling disturbance. Whilst it is true that promiscuous behaviour is also a form of searching for love and confirmation of oneself, there were not many cases reported where a firm link could be established between this sort of behaviour and the presence of a handicapped child. It is worth mentioning, however, that especially by older children attention is not always sought exclusively from the parent who originally failed to give it. Attention-seeking patterns of behaviour can carry over into later life and affect a wide variety of relationships.

6. Stealing

Just as children can turn to the 'wrong' people for the thing that
they basically want, so they can also take the 'wrong' thing.
Many examples of siblings stealing were given by caseworkers
but in fact almost all the cases of persistent stealing arose in
families where there were multiple problems of which the impact
of handicap was merely one. That childhood theft does represent
a search for a mother's love, however, has long been recognized
by child psychologists. Winnicott sums up this fact when he says:

> 'The child who is thieving is an infant looking for the mother
> or for the person from whom he has a right to steal; in fact
> he seeks the person from whom he can take things, just as,
> as an infant and a little child of one or two years old, he took
> things from his mother simply because she was his mother,
> and because he had rights over her.'

THE PAY-OFF FROM ATTENTION-SEEKING BEHAVIOUR

The implicit aim of these various behavioural 'ploys' has already
been outlined: what remains to be seen is the extent to which
they are successful, and in fact it would seem that in the majority
of cases they are not very successful at all.

One factor working against their success is that they arise
from the child's unconscious needs; they are therefore directed
towards the right psychological objective, but set about reaching
their goal in an entirely irrational way. As a result, most
attention-seeking behaviour will succeed in attracting parental
attention, but in failing to take into consideration the quality of
parental attention attracted, it will fail to meet the primary need
of the child.

Caseworkers frequently observed that many parents, far
from understanding the motives behind their child's disruptive
behaviour, view it coldly as just another problem on their already
crowded plate. 'As if I haven't got enough worries as it is!' said
one mother when her able-bodied child started truanting from
school and spending the day at home. In this case, as in many
others, the mother had altogether failed to understand the connection between the disturbed behaviour of the sibling and her
own preoccupation with the 'other worries' in her life.

The failure of parents to make connections which to an out-
sider may seem obvious is an important feature of many of the

families we are discussing. The following example illustrates the resistance that some parents have against doing this, even though on one level at least they are aware of what their able-bodied children are trying to do.

VE: In the past, the 10-year-old girl has done a little bit of stealing. She stopped this after a while because the parents got very worked up, but now she makes a sort of clicking sound in her mouth all the time when she's wanting parental attention. She tends to be left out of things because of the accent on the handicapped child. Nearly always when I'm there she does this; she'll come into the room and make this loud clicking sound to attract attention, and the parents say that she does this a lot in the evenings.

SK: Do they realize that she is doing this to attract attention?

VE: They appreciate on a general level that the younger children are certainly being left out when Sue is at home, but since Sharon has been based in hospital for the last two years they feel that the other children must have been getting all the attention they need. They realize that the acting-out of the second child is something to do with this feeling of being left out of the family, but whenever I see them they still appear to be completely absorbed with the handicapped child, and one has very deliberately to force them to look at the problems of the other children. For example, the second child is at present very anxious about moving to a new school, a secondary school, and she has brought this up more than once in interviews and been completely ignored by the mother.

We can see from this example how easily the child's aim of drawing attention to her own unmet needs can be thwarted by the parent's reluctance to see what is happening in the family as a whole. Most parents do not want to make the association between a sibling's disturbance and their own over-protective attitude towards the handicapped child, because to do so would involve an admission that they are over-protective of the handicapped child and neglectful of the sibling. This in turn would mean uncovering all the defences they have built up to cope with their ambivalent feelings about handicap. Rather than do this, they merely add to these defences by refusing to see the message which the sibling is trying to communicate; they view his behaviour superficially, in terms of its disruptive effect on themselves, as a nuisance, as naughtiness, or as a disorder which has

mysteriously arisen in the internal life of the sibling. Caseworkers described many cases where either the mother or the
father or both had 'blinkered' themselves in this way.

As a result of this tendency, siblings are not only likely to
fail in their unconscious aim of securing parental affection and
love, but their behaviour will also often have the very reverse
effect of alienating them even further from their parents. It is
a cruel irony of life for many of these children that although
from early childhood they have powerful unconscious 'mechanisms'
for defending themselves against pain and they have also the
capacity to develop a variety of 'ploys' to bring about the fulfilment of unmet needs, yet the very mechanisms and ploys to
which they turn for relief will often serve only to heighten their
pain and render less possible the chance of their needs being
met. Many families were described where attention-seeking
behaviour was dealt with by parents in a punitive way, or where
it merely exaggerated the imbalance in the distribution of
parental favour within the family.

CONCLUSION

In this chapter I have tried to show how the sibling's search for
attention is a response to his frequently unavoidable neglect
as an important member of the family. In cases where the handicapped child himself has been rejected by the family (either
implicitly or literally sent away) or where they have come to
terms with his handicap and are able to balance his needs more
fairly against those of their other children, many of the sibling
reactions I have described here will be minimized, or may not
appear at all. For the rest it seems that the underlying pattern
of neglect and response, followed perhaps by further rejection
of the sibling, is almost a universal phenomenon.

The pattern itself may be summed up by quoting the mother
of a mongol girl; she was talking at a conference on the care of
the mentally handicapped on the problems she had encountered
in bringing up her mongol child. Her only comments on her
able-bodied daughter were these:

'It will be appreciated that the time I had to spend doing things
for Jane (the handicapped child), and the help that she had to
receive all the time, meant some loss of attention for my other
daughter. I found and still find that Jane makes such demands
on my patience that I have little left for other members of the

family, and after a more than usually trying day I am apt to be impatient at the small faults and tiresomeness of my elder daughter and even my husband. It is perhaps not surprising that we had difficulties with the elder child; she became jealous and tried to be babyish to attract attention and was clearly disturbed, as the persistence of thumb-sucking, asthma, etc. confirmed. In the end we decided to send her away to boarding school - she was then eight. '

One cannot help wondering if this was, in fact, the end.

References

Bakwin, H. Pure maternal overprotection and overaffection. 'Journal of Pediatrics', vol. 33, no. 6, 1948, p.788.

Barclay, J. In 'Community care of the mentally handicapped'. Proceedings of National Conference NSMHC, 1960.

Davis, F. 'Passage Through Crisis'. Bobbs-Merrill, USA, 1963.

Donnison, D.V. 'The Neglected Child'. Manchester University Press, 1954.

Levy, D.M. 'Maternal Overprotection'. Columbia University Press, New York, 1943.

Winnicott, D.W. 'The Child and the Outside World'. Tavistock Publications, London, 1957.

7 Rivalry behaviour

'Whereas in the child's relations towards its parents love would
seem to be emotion that is usually first evoked, in its dealings
with the other junior members of the family the opposite emotion
of hate is in most cases the primary reaction.'

J.C. Flugel.

In the last chapter I looked at a situation in which the sibling's
unmet emotional needs led him to indulge in attention-seeking
behaviour. The model upon which this type of perspective is
based is essentially dyadic, in other words it is primarily con-
concerned with the interaction between two persons only. The
two persons involved in this instance are, of course, the sibling
who demands attention and the parent who withholds it.

In the present chapter I shall examine some of the ways in
which the sibling's demand for parental attention both affects and
is affected by the social organization of the family as a whole.
For although the parent/sibling dyad provides the basis for a
psychological explanation of the sibling's need-oriented behaviour,
the dyad itself may be regarded as merely one element in other
much wider systems of personal relations. In this chapter I
shall examine in particular the sibling's need for attention as a
part of the 'system' of sibling rivalry operating within the family.

THE RIVALRY SYSTEM

It is important for us to get a clear picture of what a rivalry
system is and how it works on a general level, before we look in
detail at the operation of this system in the families under study.

A parent cannot usually attend to the needs of more than one
child at a time. Every parent, therefore, operates a balance in
meeting the needs of his respective children. Time spent in
attending to the needs of one child is balanced against time spent

in attending to the needs of the others. To this extent children are rivals with each other in their bids to secure the time and affection of their parents.

Every sibling will not unnaturally have feelings of jealousy and resentment towards his rival brother or sister, and may entertain hostile thoughts or indulge in aggressive behaviour towards him. Such aggression, as one would expect, tends to increase in direct proportion to the parent's preoccupation with the other child.

In this rivalry situation we find not one dyad, but three: parent/first child, parent/second child, and first child/second child. Although on one level we can look at the interaction in any of these dyads as a separate phenomenon, on another level we can see that the interaction in each dyad bears a direct relation to what is happening in the others. The more pre-occupied the parent becomes with the first child, for example, the less preoccupied he becomes with the second, and as the balance of favour swings in this way, so the second child will become increasingly jealous and hostile towards the first. Because these separate relationships are inter-related we can describe the overall situation as a system of interaction; the rivalry system may be represented diagrammatically as follows:

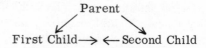

Clearly this is an oversimplified representation. In real situations the pattern will frequently be more complicated. For example there may be more than one parent-figure at the top, leading to the creation of a second pyramid, or more than two children at the bottom, resulting in a far more complex set of interdependent relationships. Nevertheless, the basic form of the pyramid remains.

Let us consider for a moment how this rivalry system works from the point of view of the children in the pyramid. The problem begins when a second child is about to be born; prior to this the firstborn is unrivalled in his demands for parental attention. With the birth of the sibling, however, he suddenly finds himself in what I have described as a rivalry situation, the most notable feature of which is his own displacement as the 'baby' of the family. The child is quite helpless and unable to control this sudden shift of parental attention to his new rival,

and the situation could be emotionally disastrous for him were it
not for the fact that the balance is restored in a number of remark-
able ways.

For a start, if his parents are good parents the child will
have shared in their joy of childbirth and also perhaps in their
sense of personal achievement. This in itself can help to redress
the balance for him, but perhaps the most important compensation lies in the fact that although the child has lost his position
in the limelight of family affairs, he will suddenly find himself
endowed with an entirely new status within the family group,
indeed one might almost say with a new identity, for he is now a
Big Brother (or Sister), with all the privilege and concession,
as well as the responsibility, that this new role implies. What
is more, this identity will be reinforced by his literal superiority,
both physically and intellectually; because this natural superiority offers him such a distinct advantage over his rival brother or
sister, the mere presence of this second child will spur him on
along his own developmental path. We can see, then, that although the first child appears to be the loser, there are, under
normal circumstances a number of physical and social compensations which serve to keep the situation in balance.

THE RIVALRY SYSTEM IN FAMILIES WITH A HANDICAPPED CHILD

Let us turn our attention back again to families in which there is
a handicapped child. In a large sample of such families we find
that although we can use the same pyramidal model to explain
what is happening there emerges a pattern which is significantly
different from the relatively balanced pattern I have just described. What tends to happen is that the parent/handicapped
child relationship strengthens in emotional intensity, leaving the
parent/sibling relationship relatively weak. Not only does the
sibling become increasingly jealous and hostile in this situation
but the parent, being overprotective of the handicapped child,
will go to greater lengths to control such jealous behaviour. On
top of this imbalance, many of the normal compensations referred
to above are denied to the sibling in these circumstances. For
one thing there is little sense of joy in which he can share when
his brother or sister is born, and he is unlikely to want to boast
to his peers about his new 'acquisition'. What is worse, whether
the handicapped child is sick or not, his special disposition tends

to override the normal privilege of the sibling, and whereas in the 'normal' family, feelings of hostility between siblings can be acted-out in play, in the 'handicapped' family, child is often separated from child, the disabled one being protected from the able-bodied. This means of course that the sibling cannot dissipate his hostile feelings through the immediate channels of interaction.

The differential treatment of sibling and handicapped child by parents was documented in a study by Shere (1956) who investigated thirty pairs of twins. Within each pair one child was cerebral-palsied. The behaviour of the parents towards the twins differed in the following respects: 1. The parents generally expected the non-cerebral palsied twin to assume more responsibilities and to act older than his age or capabilities would warrant. 2. The parents overprotected the cerebral-palsied twin, permitting him little discretion in his activities. 3. The parents tended to be more responsive to the problems of the cerebral-palsied child and oblivious of those of his twin.

These findings were borne out by caseworkers' observations in my own study. Time and again caseworkers reported an unwillingness on the part of parents to discipline their handicapped child or take a firm grip on him. Comments such as the following were all too common:

'The eldest one has leukaemia and is terminally ill. The mother here always talks as if she's afraid that the younger boy is missing out but in reality she finds it very difficult to deny the older one anything, or to discipline him - therefore he gets away with things that John, the younger one, doesn't get away with. Not surprisingly John can't understand this.'

A girl with a kidney condition is:

'.... very much treated as the baby of the family although she is fifteen. The fact that she is handicapped makes her over-protected and the centre of attention. The attitude is very much one of "Poor Elaine, she needn't have a job if she doesn't want one, she needn't go to school if she doesn't want to, I can't tell her to go to the hospital, I can't tell her not to go out. Elaine must do as she likes because poor Elaine is ill." And of course Elaine plays up to this. She is intelligent and she can manipulate people.'

In his study of the families of polio victims, Davis also noticed this imbalance in the system of reward and punishment in the family. Talking of the return of the handicapped child from hospital, he says (p. 119):

'Characteristically, his return occasioned in the family what may be termed a state of socio-political imbalance, especially as regards the nature and exercise of parental authority and the behavioural norms that govern sibling relations. The absence of the sick child from the family circle had permitted the parents to pursue different, and often contradictory, policies towards him and his siblings.'

And later, more explicitly, he says (p. 125):

'Regardless of the particular balance or style of rewards and punishments that had been employed by the parents prior to the child's illness, he was invariably subjected to a different pattern of discipline following his return from the hospital. This always tended in the direction of less frequent and less severe forms of punishment, greater toleration for a wider range of misbehaviours, and, in general, a more indulgent and compromising response to the child's conduct.'

When handicapped children discover this sort of parental 'weakness' they naturally try to exploit it. The following caseworker's description of a four-year-old shows how easily this can be done:

'He is thoroughly spoilt and he knows just how to play up to his mother. If he gets ticked off, he immediately begins rolling his eyes around and pretending he's going to go into another attack.... the other children in the nursery don't let him play up so much, they just give him a wallop if he is being difficult, but his mother never fails to give in. In fact he knows exactly who he can play up and he tests people out.'

The sibling in such families, then, is fighting against unfair odds. Regardless of age he is the one who is 'normal', the one who is expected to 'understand' and 'make allowances' for his handicapped brother or sister. It is not always realized that these allowances are often made at his own expense. As a caseworker said of one family who had been living for three years under the threat of the imminent death of a boy with leukaemia, the chances were ten to one in any dispute between the children that the handicapped child would win. And in another family where Helen, the oldest, was mongoloid, the worker observed that:

'If Helen wants something from Gillian her mother always
says "let her have it", just to keep the peace, and of course
she mustn't argue with Helen. She can argue to a certain
extent but then her mother will tell her to stop, to let Helen
have her own way.'

We can see without any great difficulty that the rivalry pyramid
in such families is lop-sided. What is happening in terms of our
rivalry diagram is that one of the two sets of arrows, which represent opposing forces normally held in balance, is here being
systematically invalidated. The handicapped child in fact has
won the rivalry battle, hands down.

Jealousy

This imbalance in the rivalry system leads to powerful feelings
of jealousy on the part of the 'losing' sibling, such feelings being
directed towards the more successful brother or sister. One
caseworker said:

'I used to feel almost embarrassed when both children were
present during interviews. Little Richard was so patently
jealous of his sister that it was painful to watch. He would sit
on the edge of his chair and whenever his mother mentioned
Carol's name......oh, Carol does this or Carol's having
trouble with that, he would butt in and say what he had done
and what he was having trouble with. And even when he was
doing something else and you thought he wasn't listening he
would turn round whenever Carol was mentioned and throw in
some remark about himself.'

Jealousy differs from attention-seeking behaviour in that it is
essentially hostile in intention, whereas the latter is concerned
only with reclaiming what it has lost. Its motivating force is the
desire to destroy the envied person, at least to the extent that
he possesses some coveted object or quality; attention-seeking
behaviour, on the other hand, seeks only to reclaim the object
of envy, the love to which the child lays a natural and rightful
claim. Many caseworkers noted this element of hostility between
siblings. Sometimes it was seen in terms of sly digs and pokes
or endless attempts to get the other child into trouble. In other
cases the respective children had nothing whatever to do with
each other:

'...It's as if he doesn't exist for Paul. They can be in the same room together and there's never a word between them. If you ask him what he thinks about Paul he'll say "nothing" and change the subject. But it's not a complete indifference: there's a feeling of bitterness behind it.'

Marcia was an eleven-year-old girl whose severely handicapped sister had been placed in residential care but remained very much at the centre of family life:

'Marcia said that she had been very glad when Julie went away to school because when she had been at home she screamed and always knocked things over and spoilt things. When I asked her how she spoilt things she cited one specific incident which she obviously still felt very bitter about. On this occasion Julie had knocked over a bottle of milk, but she, not Julie, had been blamed and punished by the parents. Marcia then said without any prompting that Julie got all the attention of her parents. I asked her if she tried to get attention herself and she replied with a coy smile, "Yes, by screaming and getting into a temper". She then went on to make it quite clear that she "hated Julie in every way". She said she used to feel like hitting her, especially when her parents bought new clothes and presents for Julie and not for herself, but she never actually did hit her.'

A number of interesting things stand out in this report. Asked how the handicapped child spoilt things for her, Marcia replied very clearly in terms of the effect on her own relationship with her parents; she had been blamed and punished by them. Moreover, the issue here is not merely one of injustice in an isolated incident, a fact which Marcia herself underlines by adding that Julie gets all the attention of her parents. The issue she is raising concerns the overall imbalance of the rivalry system within her family. We notice in this context that not only does she strive to attract the attention of her parents, she is also understandably jealous of the sister who is more successful in attracting their attention than she herself is. I would venture to suggest that such feelings are the rule rather than the exception amongst siblings of the handicapped.

The truth of this has been borne out in group work with siblings. Some evidence has also been obtained from question-naire surveys in the East Midlands. Sheila Hewett conducted a survey of 180 families with a cerebral-palsied child under the age of eight. Of those mothers who had at least one other child in their family, 33 per cent reported that the sibling was jealous of his handicapped brother or sister. In a London-based survey by Joan McMichael 35 per cent of mothers of children with mixed handicaps reported that the sibling was jealous of the handicapped child.

Questionnaire surveys such as these have serious limitations and there are a number of reasons why we should regard these figures as underestimates. For a start, both surveys were based on single interviews with only one parent. Brief interviews may be adequate for obtaining certain sorts of information, but it has been the repeated experience of caseworkers and other investigators (Davis pp 115-116) that many mothers are unwilling to admit to 'cracks' in family life, such as jealousy between siblings until a relationship of trust has been built up with the person asking the questions. Mothers naturally want to present their families, and their own ability to cope, in the best possible light.

A second reason why we may regard these figures as underestimates is that the percentages given include families where the siblings were extremely young. For example, none of the siblings in McMichael's sample was considered too young to rate for jealousy, and only eight 'infants' out of Hewett's sample of 180 families were considered too young. But leading child psychologists such as Gesell have shown that children do not have the social awareness to have feelings of jealousy towards another child before the age of about two and a half or three. The ages of Hewett's and McMichael's siblings were not given, but in view of the ages of the handicapped children (all eight years and under) many siblings must have been included who were really too young to be showing signs of jealousy.

A final reason why these figures are likely to be underestimates is that the samples on which the studies were based consisted of handicapped children living at home (Hewett), and handicapped children attending a day school (McMichael). Both samples are therefore likely to be biased towards the inclusion of the more mildly handicapped. There is mounting evidence that the more mildly handicapped the child, the less his effect will be on the able-bodied sibling (Farber, 1965.). All these factors point to the same conclusion as was reached by McMichael, that 'The figures tend to underestimate the extent of the problem.'

Absence of jealousy

Of course not all siblings display jealousy towards their handicapped brothers and sisters and there are many reasons why
this is so. In some families, for example, the rivalry system
is not imbalanced in the way that I have described, and I will be
looking at the way these families have managed to maintain their
equilibrium in a later chapter. There are also some families
where there is an imbalance, but where the sibling is able to
find the affection he needs either from the second parent or else
from another parent-figure such as a grandmother or family
friend. Again, there are some families in which the siblings are
so far apart in age that they do not pose a threat to each other as
rivals for attention. Indeed the further apart in age the sibling
was from his handicapped brother or sister, the less frequently
were signs of disturbance reported by caseworkers.

Quite apart from all these straightforward exceptions, however, there remain many families of the sort referred to, where
the rivalry system is clearly imbalanced, yet where the siblings,
although relatively close in age to the handicapped child, do not
outwardly appear to be jealous of him. What has happened in
these families? Is there perhaps something special about the
child which absolves him from the feeling of jealousy or does he
experience feelings of jealousy which are subsequently brought
under some sort of control?

I would argue that the second of these hypotheses comes
closer to the truth and that the jealous behaviour of the sibling
is frequently controlled or socialized by the parent in such a
way that it cannot easily be identified.

Disguised jealousy

There is in fact a great deal of evidence to support this hypothesis, for with every case of the outright expression of jealousy
mentioned by caseworkers there was at least one case of what
appeared to be disguised jealousy, and for every case of this,
there was a case of something even more controlled, which often
appears at first to be the very reverse of jealousy, but the origin
of which was all too clear on closer observation.

Let us look at some descriptions of such behaviour, beginning with a family of three in which the youngest child has spina
bifida:

WK: The second child is showing a lot of disguised jealousy towards the third.

SK: Can you elaborate a little more on that - what sort of disguised jealousy is it?

WK: Well, for example, she will help her mother to look after the spina bifida child, but, at the same time she will upset the chair on which he is sitting or upset the pram, and on several occasions the spina bifida boy has rolled out on to the floor and hurt himself because of this girl. She is very clumsy in her handling of him, which is quite unnecessary because in every other thing she is not clumsy in her movements. She plays the piano very well; she's a very graceful child in other respects. The mother creates this problem because she is so very over-protective of the boy. She spoils him completely and she doesn't hide this at all in front of the other children. I think on many occasions she is very unfair to them and this contributes to the girl's jealousy.

We find a similar ambivalence in siblings of all ages; in the next case the girl was much older, aged seventeen:

> 'She pours "love" on to the handicapped child, feels guilty whe
> he is away, yet won't bring her friends home when he is there,
> mainly I think because she is a little bit ashamed. She also
> talks a lot about wishing she had normal brothers and sisters,
> but at the same time when the sister's there she will wait on
> her hand and foot.'

And the same ambivalence can be seen in a nine-year-old boy:

> 'His behaviour is quite inconsistent. On the one hand he appea
> to be very affectionate towards Marlene, his handicapped
> sister; he'll pat her and cuddle her but then when his mother's
> back is turned you'll see him suddenly get in a very sly dig or
> deliberately squeeze her extra hard. Underneath his affection
> he's basically very jealous, but he's frightened to express it.'

We find in all of these cases that feelings of jealousy and hostility are being covered up by the child. There can be no doubt that disguised or ambivalent feelings such as these are largely a product of socialization - that is, the social control of behaviou which the parent, for reasons which by now should be obvious, either does not approve of or cannot accept. It is true that there are many other agents of socialization within the child's environ-

92

ment, but the parent is undoubtedly the most powerful and significant of these if only because it is the parent upon whom the child
is emotionally dependent throughout its formative years. Why,
then, does a sibling need to disguise the jealousy he feels? The
answer, surely, is that the parent who is naturally defensive
and overprotective of the handicapped child will not readily
tolerate any overt expression of jealousy on the part of the sibling.
The sibling, for his part, will soon learn that the more he ex-
presses feelings of jealousy towards his handicapped rival, the
more he will be alienated from his parents, and this is something he cannot afford to do. Because acceptance by his parents
is so vitally important to him, he will be strongly motivated to
modify his behaviour in the ways that they desire.

Different theoretical standpoints could be taken to explain
this phenomenon in a variety of ways. A learning theorist for
example, would locate the source of the parent's power in his
capacity to reward and punish the child. The child is rewarded
by any parental action which indicates feelings of love and acceptance; he is punished by any parental action which indicates lack
of concern or rejection. Reward in this sense is conceived not
merely as some sort of bonus for the child, but as the fulfilment
of his most basic needs. In this way the parent can be said to
'reinforce' the behaviour he desires from the child by rewarding
or punishing him at appropriate times.

Those taking a psychoanalytic standpoint would be more
likely to explain the same thing in terms of the sibling's 'identification' with the parent. We have already seen how the sibling
is frequently neglected, and as Anthony Storr points out:

'The fear of being abandoned leads to an attempt to re-identify
with the parents and to an introjection of their standards and
attitudes - in other words, to the establishment of that internal
and primitive type of conscience which psychoanalysis has made
familiar as the super-ego.'

Whichever approach we choose to take, the outcome is the same,
namely that the forces at work upon the child all urge him to
adopt a similar attitude to that of his parents, and to behave in a
similar way.

THE INTERNALIZATION OF WELFARE NORMS

The attitude of parents is, as we have seen, most commonly one

of concern and overprotection. It is not surprising, then, to
find so many siblings repressing their jealousy, if only partially,
and behaving in an affectionate way with the handicapped child.
This after all is what their parents do and what their parents
encourage them to do. In this way they can find a viable solution
to the rivalry problem by doing what the old adage says: 'if you
can't beat 'em, join 'em'. The sibling thus comes a little closer
to his parents and is able to win their approval by adopting the
same behaviour as they display towards the handicapped child.
At least one investigator believes that this process of adaptation
goes even further than I have suggested. M.A. Strauss conducted a series of interviews with mothers of retarded children
and came to the conclusion that:

> 'sustained interaction with retarded siblings comes to be
> regarded as a duty by the normal siblings and in the perform-
> ance of this duty the normal sibling internalizes welfare norms
> and turns his life career towards the improvement of mankind,
> or at least towards goals requiring dedication and sacrifice.'

There is no doubt that things are neither as simple nor as absolute
as Strauss would seem to suggest. It would be ridiculous, for
example, to assume that every sibling reacts in the way he describes. Nevertheless his conclusions contain more than an
element of truth, for in many families the socialization of the
sibling's rivalry behaviour is without question carried beyond his
relation to the handicapped child in his own family to a general
internalization of welfare norms.

One family where we can see very clearly how this has
happened is the Grant family. The handicapped child, and indeed
the very concept of handicap, lie very much at the centre of all
activities in this family. One can see here that the sibling is in
a position of having to adopt her parents' preoccupation with
handicap if she wishes to be accepted as a person in her own
right:

PA: The handicapped child here is nine; she is of at least
average intelligence, but is very deaf, and has only just started
to walk. I think the older child has always had to do far too much
for Elizabeth, the handicapped girl. The mother here is very
good with Elizabeth and is very warm and affectionate with her,
but she soon reaches the point where she has to go away and be
on her own, and then the older child has to take over as mother.
The older girl is now doing her CSEs and is about to leave

school, and she wants to work with handicapped children. I asked her on one occasion why she wanted to work with handicapped children, and she said 'because I owe them so much'.

SK: What do you think she meant by that?

PA: I wasn't able to pursue it on that occasion because Mum came back at that point, but I think she meant that she was desperately guilty, because she wasn't handicapped herself, and although she's given so much to Elizabeth, she hasn't worked through her feelings about her and she wants to continue working-through them in terms of working with handicapped children. She spends a lot of her spare time in a local nursery for handicapped children when she isn't at home looking after Elizabeth.

SK: Do you feel that this is something that the mother has forced on to her in terms of making her look after Elizabeth so much?

PA: I think the mother pushed a lot of responsibility on to her, but I wouldn't use the word forced because it seemed to be very willingly accepted. I've been there when both children were there, and Elizabeth has really been bloody-minded towards Annette, she says, 'do this and do that' and Annette never says shut up, or no. Elizabeth is very demanding and I think because she's a bright child, she is more frustrated by her handicap than a less-bright child would be, and therefore she's even more demanding when she's at home.

SK: And have the family re-adjusted themselves around her, to the extent that they accept all her demands?

PA: Yes, they accept her demands for the weekends when she is at home, and then, of course, they relax during the week when she's back at school. By the end of the long holidays they're all laid out, they're so exhausted and Annette more so than anybody.

SK: So when she's home she's really the centre of attention.

PA: Yes, absolutely.

SK: Do you think that the only way the older child can approach the mother is through the handicapped child since the mother spends so much time and attention with her?

PA: That's interesting – I hadn't thought of that. You may absolutely have put your finger on it. I think you have. I have been bothered about the relationship between the mother and the elder girl. Annette quite often comes home from school in the middle of my visits and there always seems something strained about the way they talk to each other. It's something you notice immediately. The mother never seems to care about the girl being back from school. Yes, it may be that she can't approach her mother directly, and that in fact this is the only way she can make contact, through the little one, and the mother does have a very spontaneous relation with the handicapped girl, she's very warm with her and understands her very well and of course she's preoccupied with her. So this may well be what's happening here.

SK: How does the father fit in here? Is he in the picture at all?

PA: Yes, but he opts out insofar as he spends all of his spare time, or at least a very large part of it in raising funds for the local handicapped children's fund. Night after night he's in his room preparing Christmas cards, and all sorts of things like this. He runs fetes, and all this, in addition to his ordinary work. He's nice to talk to, he's a very pleasant charming man, he's also very warm with Elizabeth, and yet he opts out in this particular sense. I think that Elizabeth is very much the focal point of this family, even though she's not there for five days a week. The mother also does fund-raising for the local group. She runs coffee mornings and that sort of thing, although not as much as the father. So of course she doesn't object to what he's doing.

This case illustrates many of the points I have been making in this chapter. We are not told here whether the sibling was ever overtly jealous, although there is a good deal of evidence from other case records to suppose that she was. What we can see, however, is that the relation between the girl and her mother is at best 'strained' and that the girl is in a situation where she is very clearly 'rewarded' for repressing her jealousy and for adopting instead a motherly approach. She would undoubtedly be 'punished' (in the sense referred to above) for openly expressing her jealousy in this sort of family, and all in all she has a very big incentive for what Strauss called internalizing welfare norms.

WHAT HAPPENS TO FEELINGS OF HOSTILITY?

So far I have examined a number of strands in those processes of socialization that affect the sibling's relation to a handicapped brother or sister. I have argued amongst other things that there is a marked imbalance in the rivalry system in families where there is a handicapped child, and that in such families the sibling's feelings of jealousy and hostility are naturally exacerbated. I have further suggested that there are strong forces at work which are conducive to the control of such feelings. These forces originate both within the parent, who has an instinctive desire to protect the handicapped child and control the sibling's negative feelings towards him, and within the sibling, who has a desperate need to win the approval of his parents, having already lost a great deal of their attention to the handicapped child.

There is a well-established theory of aggression which stresses the fact that although feelings of aggression can be controlled, they cannot easily be 'extinguished' altogether. One well-known psychiatrist (Storr, 1971) has written of this emotion that:

'Of all human tendencies aggression, in particular, is hidden, disguised, side-tracked, ascribed to outside agencies, and when it appears it is always a difficult task to trace it to its origins.'

A man may have a frustrating day at the office and 'work off his aggression' in the car going home, or else he may kick the dog when really it is the next-door neighbour who has aroused his anger. His aggression in both cases has been displaced from an object towards which he knows he must control his anger (the office, the neighbour), on to an object which is 'safe' (the car, the dog).

A number of caseworkers drew attention to a similar process at work amongst siblings. They pointed out that their aggression and jealousy were being displaced in ways which were relatively 'safe'. Any channel might be considered safe in this context so long as it does not directly threaten the sibling's relationship with his mother and father. There are enough convincing examples to suggest that this process is in fact a very common one, although notably more examples can be cited of boys displacing aggression than girls. (Perhaps this is merely a sign that boys express their aggression in different ways from girls.)

What stands out in the examples that follow is the frequency with which the sibling's 'affection' towards his handicapped brother or sister was felt to be somehow not quite real or else not consistent with the sibling's overall behaviour. This observation, however, was not always linked by the caseworker with those acts of aggression which I am suggesting are displacement activities.

In the Hicks family there were two severely handicapped children, both with progressive conditions. The caseworker described their nine-year-old brother in the following way:

CS: He has started to bully younger children outside the family and other mothers have been complaining to her that 'her Tim has been bashing up their kids'. He has just started doing this. It might be because he is not getting much attention from his mother. She says she doesn't have the time to provide this as she has to spend such a lot of time with these two that are dying and need everything doing for them - I mean literally everything, they just lie on a couch all day.

Later in this interview I asked 'how does he react to these handicapped children. Is he jealous?' The answer was as follows:

CS: I don't know. His reaction is that he goes up to the handicapped children and kisses them and kisses them, and all this sort of thing which his mother obviously approves of.

SK: What, genuinely kisses them and shows them affection?

CS: I don't know. He doesn't do anything for them, just comes in and kisses them and then really ignores them after that. It's rather funny. Of course, mother insists that he isn't worried or bothered by them at all - or she did do, right up until this bullying started.

In the next example there are again two handicapped children in the family; but in this one there were four siblings, two of whom were in all sorts of trouble.

MB: Well, they had quite a normal family of four children, and then just one after another they had these two handicapped children, and it just altered the whole family outlook. But in fact they all seem to get on very well with the two handicapped children, especially the eldest girl, and when she was running away from home and threatening suicide and all this sort of thing she said this was the one thing that kept her and made her come back because she was so fond of her two handicapped sisters. This also applied to the eldest boy, who was very delinquent. He was expelled from his school and was on probation for stealing. He was also very aggressive – he nearly killed a boy once, he knocked him over and banged the back of his head on the pavement.

SK: But towards the handicapped children he was affectionate?

MB: He was very affectionate. He used to meet them from school, he used to stay at home to look after them and he didn't mind at all.

Finally, the same pattern can be seen to apply to a younger child, Ted, who is only five years old. His younger brother was cerebral palsied.

MB: There are two boys here, Nick and Ted. The disturbance here arose because Ted was replaced as the baby of the family by this little spastic boy. Of course he really did need more attention than a normal child would, although I don't think Ted could realize this. As far as he was concerned here was some-one screaming for his mother's attention and she was giving it to him. He himself was missing out, and as a result was very jealous and naughty. He has just started school and I hear he has been very aggressive at school. He's also been thrown out of Sunday school.

SK: How does he behave towards the handicapped child?

MB: Well, he hates him, and he's obviously jealous of him, but for some reason he's never openly spiteful to him, in fact rather the reverse. The mother herself has mentioned this because recently she's been talking a lot about this child and how aggressive he's been at school.

What I would suggest has happened in these cases, and in others like them, is that the sibling has redirected his hostile feelings, which were initially aroused by the handicapped child, towards other more 'neutral' children. This happens because the price of being openly aggressive towards the favoured handicapped child is, or can be, simply too high to pay.

CONCLUSION

This chapter has been necessarily biased. I began by proposing a general model by means of which different forms of rivalry behaviour could be explained. I then concentrated on only one of these forms: the one which appeared to be by far the most common in families with both a handicapped and an able-bodied child. Here, as elsewhere, I have not attempted to state the position of every sibling of every handicapped child, but merely to point out what is the common experience of many such siblings.

There are many important variables which play their part in determining the response of any given child. The sex of both handicapped child and sibling; the age gap between the two; whether the sibling is born before or after the handicapped child; the number of other siblings in the family; the way in which the rivalry system is modified in families of different sorts and sizes; the nature and severity of disability suffered; the degree to which the handicapped child is dependent on others – all of these variables will affect the sibling's response and all are therefore important.

What is clear is that throughout the spectrum of different possibilities, whether the sibling is young or old, boy or girl, born before or after the handicapped child, he frequently finds himself in a system of sibling rivalry which is heavily biased against him. Indeed, so strong are the forces working to protect and succour the handicapped child that even the sibling's feelings of jealousy towards him may be strongly controlled or suppressed.

References

Davis, F. 'Passage through Crisis'. Bobbs-Merrill, USA, 1963.

Farber, B. Effects of severely mentally retarded children on family relations. 'Mental Retardation Abstracts', vol. 11, 1965, pp 1-17.

Flugel, J.C. 'The Psychoanalytic Study of the Family'. Hogarth Press, 1921.

Hewett, S. 'Handicapped Children and their Families'. University of Nottingham Press, 1970.

McMichael, J. 'Handicap : a Study of Physically Handicapped Children and their Families'. Staples Press, London, 1971.

Secord, P. and Backman, C. 'Social Psychology'. McGraw Hill, 1964.

Shere, M. Socio-emotional factors in the family of twins with cerebral palsy. 'Exceptional Children', No. 22, 1956, p 196.

· Rivalry behaviour

Strauss, M.A. Interaction with retarded siblings and life-goals
    of children. 'Marriage and Family Living, No. 25, 1963,
    pp 96-98.

Storr, A. 'Human Aggression'. Penguin, London, 1971.

8 Attitudes to death

To children who have progressive and incurable diseases, and also to their families, death is an ever-present reality. It is hard to determine the exact number of children who die as a direct or an indirect result of congenital or acquired diseases, even though the official statistics on this are rather more complete than they are for disability itself. One thing, however, is certain: death is no stranger to families of the severely handicapped. The sibling's response to death is therefore a factor which cannot be overlooked in a study such as this.

Unfortunately, all the families I originally chose to discuss with caseworkers had both a handicapped child and at least one able-bodied sibling in them. I therefore inadvertently omitted families where the handicapped child had already died. Of the remaining cases there were a few, however, in which a child did die in the time that elapsed between sending out the questionnaires and the detailed discussion of cases with the workers concerned. The effect of the death on the siblings in these families was immediately apparent, and I therefore sought to supplement these cases with other material which was subsequently brought forward by caseworkers, and by the results of a number of prominent studies both in this country and in the United States which have been undertaken in the last few years.

All of this material confirms beyond doubt that the death of a handicapped child poses a very considerable strain on a sibling and can be a source of lasting distress. There is also a growing body of evidence to suggest that a child's response to the death of a handicapped sibling differs in a number of notable ways from his response to the deaths of other persons, such as his parents. To understand why these responses differ is important not only for those who work with families in which there is a handicapped child, but also for the more general enlargement of our concepts of grief-reaction and bereavement in childhood.

As with many of the responses I have described, the child's response to the death of a handicapped sibling is not invariant. The way in which any particular child responds will depend upon a variety of factors.

Maria Nagy, for example, has demonstrated that a child's age has an important effect on his ability to understand what death actually is. She has shown that children under the age of about nine years do not have a fully developed concept of death. It is, of course, true that even an adult's ideas about death may change or develop in the light of new experiences as he grows older, but what Nagy discovered is that the young child is unable to grasp the basic concept of death, he cannot for example understand the essential fact that death means the end of one's personal and bodily functions.

Nagy observed over three hundred bereaved children and came to the conclusion that the child's concept of death passes through two developmental stages before he can understand such elementary 'facts'. In the first stage, when the child is between three and five years old, he cannot conceive of death as a regular and final process but views it instead as a departure, a further form of existence but in changed circumstances. Consequently he may talk of death as if it is a temporary state of affairs, or as if there are varying degrees of death. Thus a child of this age may accept that a person is 'very dead' but still expect him eventually to return. The child's knowledge of the outside world at this age is coloured by his own egocentrism. Nagy maintains that just as the child himself is living, and is able to experience himself as living, he perceives everything outside him as also being alive, even the dead.

In the second stage, between the approximate ages of five and nine, the child is more able to think of death as a process, but it is a process in which death itself is personified. If death exists in a general way, there must be a death-man or bogeyman who actually 'does' it.

It is only when the child is about nine years old that he can view death as a process within the individual marking the dissolution of bodily life. At this age he is able to construct logical or semi-logical explanations of how death happens, with reference to relevant biological facts. 'It's when a person doesn't live any more.' 'You stop breathing and your heart stops beating.'

It is worth noting that the same three cognitive stages in a child's understanding of death were discovered by Sylvia Anthony in a completely independent programme of research. Anthony correlated these three stages to the same approximate age-groupings : five and under, six to nine, and nine plus. She also discovered that regardless of age, children frequently referred to death, killings and similar subjects in their everyday conversation. In one experiment she asked 100 children to complete a story, the opening of which was read to them. Although death was not mentioned or implied in any of the openings some fifty per cent of the children referred to it in the course of their story.

We can conclude from this that although death is a word in the vocabulary of even very young children, the child's conception of what death is, and therefore his response to the reality of an actual death, is very much dependent on age.

There are, of course, many factors other than age upon which his response is also dependent. Cain, Fast and Erikson have the following to say in this respect :

'Reviewing the clinical data, the determinants of children's responses to the death of a sibling were found to include - the nature of the death, the age and characteristics of the child who died; the child's degree of actual involvement in his sibling's death; the child's pre-existing relationship to the dead sibling; the immediate impact of the death upon the parents; the parent's handling of the initial reactions of the surviving child; the reactions of the community; the death's impact upon the family structure; the availability to the child and the parents of various "substitutes"; the parent's enduring reactions to the child's death; the major concurrent stresses upon the child and his family; and the developmental level of the surviving child at the time of the death.'

The authors point out, moreover, that :

'The effects upon the child obviously are not static; but undergo constant developmental transformation and evolution.'

Clearly, I cannot hope to examine all of these variables or do full justice to the complexity of such responses in a single chapter. Once again, therefore, I shall merely present here the most salient variables as they appear from the case material available to me and insofar as they are supported by the work of other investigators.

Omnipotence of thought

Having viewed the handicapped child as a rival to his able-bodied sibling, and having identified the feelings of hostility and jealousy that often permeate the relationship between them, one might be tempted to think that the death of a handicapped child comes as a welcome relief to its sibling. In some ways, of course, it might, but it would be very far from the truth to suppose that the child is therefore emotionally untroubled.

In fact, a great deal of sibling disturbance seems to arise following the death of a handicapped child for the very reason that the sibling does have rivalry-bred hostile feelings which are often extremely intense. Because his most hostile wishes have been suddenly fulfilled in the death of his sibling, the young child may sometimes assume that the power of his own thoughts has actually been the cause of the death.

A child's tendency to think that his wishes have the power to influence events without physical intervention has been described by Freud as 'omnipotence of thought', and Piaget arrived at the similar concept of 'efficacy' following his own observational studies. That omnipotence of thought is frequently to be found amongst siblings of children who die was firmly established by Cain et al. (1964) and is borne out by the work of Cobb (1956), Orbach (1959), Koch (1960) and a number of other researchers.

What actually happens to a child who feels that his own jealousy or anger have directly caused the death of a brother or sister? We can probably best answer this question by looking at actual case studies. The following case was cited by Sula Wolff from her chapter on bereavement in 'Children Under Stress'.

'Allan, a five-year-old boy, had been deserted by his father in infancy. His mother had then married a farmer and there was now a step-brother aged two. Allan adored his step-father, and one day he was running to join him in the lambing-shed. The younger brother followed. Allan shouted back at him to stay behind, as he himself climbed over a low wall to reach the shed. The brother, however, toddled after him over the wall, fell into a well and was drowned. Allan's behaviour now changed completely. He became a very aggressive child, frequently in fights with other children at school and unable to concentrate on his lessons. He climbed dangerously and sustained several bad falls so that his mother was constantly afraid he would seriously injure himself. To the psychiatrist who spoke to him then and later, he revealed the recollection of his brother's death. He was able to remember the event in great detail when he was ten years old and the steady conviction that he had been responsible for the baby's death never left him. This feeling of guilt which he carried about with him for many years he was not able to discuss with his parents. He felt he must not upset his mother by 'reminding' her of the baby. She never talked of him and Allan felt he could not do so either. He wanted her to forget the child and its death although he himself could not. His guilt makes sense in terms of his repressed jealousy towards his brother who was a rival for the affection of his step-father, affection of which he was not absolutely sure. "He's not my real father but he does love me just the same." The baby died and Allan felt that his own wish to prevent the brother from joining him with the step-father in the lambing shed was responsible for the child's death. The only way in which Allan could get relief from his guilt was by inviting punishments and hurts from outside. He became naughty in school and was constantly in trouble. He became accident prone. '

As the caseworker concerned points out, what happened to the child here is essentially a guilt-reaction. The conviction that he has caused the death is in fact a corollary of the child's guilt concerning the hostile wishes and fantasies he entertained towards his brother when he was still alive. The sort of guilt that motivates irrational convictions of this kind was found by Cain to be 'rawly directly present' in at least half of the cases he encountered. In these cases, it should be remembered, there was none of the increased hostility and jealousies engendered by one of the siblings being disabled. One might reasonably expect guilt reactions to be even more frequently present, therefore, amongst siblings of the disabled after the disabled child has died.

There are many other examples of a sibling's guilt leading, through omnipotence of thought, to the conviction that he is personally responsible for the death of the disabled child. In one rather unusual case the situation was reversed. Here a little girl was in reality responsible for her brother's death, having knocked over an oil heater which resulted in a serious fire. Some years later her parents gave birth to another child who happened to be born with a congenital deformity. The girl remained convinced for many years that this deformity, like the death of her brother, was entirely her responsibility.

Feelings of guilt which are aroused by the death of a sibling can be expressed in many ways. Some children feel that they should have died along with their sibling or, perhaps, instead of him. Some have suicidal thoughts or dwell on all the nasty things they have done to the sibling in the past; others, as Cain observed, react with 'depressive withdrawals, accident-prone behaviour, punishment seeking, constant provocative testing, exhibitionistic use of guilt and grief, massive projections of super-ego accusations and many forms of acting out'. Furthermore Sylvia Anthony gives examples of children who live in fear of retaliatory punishment for having killed the sibling, if only in thought.

Parental imposition of guilt

There can be no doubt, then, that guilt is likely to play a major part in the child's reaction to a sibling's death, all the more so when the sibling in question is disabled. Although guilt is a rather covert and intangible emotion for an observer to come to grips with, it is often all too clear how it is being promoted, even though it may prove difficult to dispel.

In quite a number of cases, for example, a feeling of guilt was actually imposed by the parents on the able-bodied child following the death of the disabled sibling. This was usually unintentional on the part of the parents and arose not because they blamed the child in any overt way for the death, but simply because they failed to understand the meaning of the child's reaction to death. Many children, especially those under the age of nine, do not react in a visibly 'emotional' way as an adult might expect. Indeed it is quite normal for a young child to continue with his usual routine of eating, sleeping and playing as if nothing had happened, provided he is not unduly troubled by the reaction of others. It is only after a period of time, and perhaps after many question and answer sessions, that the real nature of the loss is felt by the child.

This reaction is clearly consistent with the child's developmental understanding of death as outlined above. It is not difficult, however, to understand why the bereaved parent, perhaps torn by feelings of guilt himself, is unable to tolerate such apparent lack of feeling on the part of the sibling. This at any rate is what caseworkers felt was happening in certain families: the child being reprimanded for his 'absence of grief' by overwrought parents. The child in this situation is unnecessarily made to feel guilty for reasons he cannot properly understand.

In some cases the parent's conviction that the sibling 'does not care' may be pushed to an extreme and become eventually a well-established pattern of belief. The unfortunate sibling may then be charged with not having done enough for the disabled child when he was alive and remarks may be made to this effect whenever the subject of the deceased child arises. It does not seem to be often, however, that parents displace their own feelings of guilt so completely on to the sibling in this way.

The taboo on death

It has often been said that death is one of the few taboo subjects left in our society; the almost universal reluctance of parents to discuss the cause, nature and implications of death openly with their children would certainly seem to bear this out. Many reasons are given by parents for this reluctance. Some regard their children as far too vulnerable to be told the truth; they feel that letting the child talk openly would merely make him more upset. Others take the opposite view, that the child is far too young to understand anyway, so there is little point in offering explanations. Whatever reason parents give, caseworkers frequently find them all too willing to brush the subject aside with hasty assurances that everything is all right, or else with fanciful and unhelpful explanations whose only real purpose is an evasive one.

Once again, this 'finding' is supported by other research. Marris discovered that 'most mothers thought it best to shield their children from the rituals surrounding death'. He found amazingly that only one in ten of the children in his random sample of bereaved families attended the funeral of the deceased.

The taboo which gives rise to this sort of 'shielding' is almost always mixed with parental ambivalence, guilt or conflict which has not yet been properly resolved. There can be little doubt that it is these things, which are after all secondary factors in the chain of events, rather than the primary factor of the death itself, which are most likely to seriously disturb the surviving child.

One family, in a singularly misguided attempt to shield their child from the reality of death, told her that her little brother had gone away for a long holiday, whereas in fact he had died. The girl, undoubtedly realizing this story was not quite the whole truth, became very distraught whenever the brother was mentioned or, more frequently, whenever he was not mentioned at times when he should have been. She jealously guarded his room, letting nobody enter it 'while he was away'. The parents although acting under the guise of protecting their daughter from pain were in reality unable to face up to the truth themselves. It took them many weeks before they were able to hold any sort of conversation about their deceased son; in that time the daughter, far from being protected, was herself subjected to an invidious fear and anxiety about the mysterious holiday of her brother and the unspeakable circumstances that surrounded his disappearance.

Situations like this, where fear is openly present but the truth remains firmly suppressed, are fertile breeding grounds for the wildest fantasies of the child. Fantasies which often exceed in intensity anything likely to be experienced if the child is exposed to the truth in an understanding way.

The distortion and suppression of reality is so often done in the alleged interest of the child that it is worth citing another case where the consequences of 'doctoring' the truth for the child are quite clear. In this case the mother complained that her four-year-old son would not go to sleep at night and in addition demanded that all the windows in his room be kept locked, even though it was the middle of summer. The boy refused to go across open streets and on the occasions when he could be persuaded to go outside at all, was unwilling to leave the shade of trees. In discussion with the parents it was revealed that when his younger brother had died he had been given the following explanation of the event, that God had reached down from heaven and while his brother slept had picked him up and taken him to heaven. There had been no further discussion either with the child or in front of him about the little brother's death; the subject was, in fact, taboo. The bewildered child was simply left to make what he could out of this 'child's version' of death. Little wonder then that he lived in fear of God reaching down a second time to pluck him also from the safety of his home.

It would be wrong to assume that the child's fears and anxieties in this sort of case arise exclusively out of the parents' reluctance to discuss the subject of death. But there can be no doubt that fears of this sort can be allayed to a very large extent by more honest and informative discussion with the child about the basic what's and why's of death and the feelings it has aroused. Provided, of course, this is done with sensitivity to the nature of the child's fears and with due regard to the limits of his understanding.

Other sources of the fear of death

There is more than a hint of identification in the sort of case I have just described. The sibling identifies with his disabled brother and thus comes to expect that the strange visitor, death, will return for him as well. Some children live in fear on this account. One seven-year-old girl refused to go to bed in the room she had previously shared with her disabled sister. She was frightened the 'bogeyman' would take her away just as he had taken away her sister during the night. Another, whose brother had died in hospital, developed an uncontrollable fear of hospitals and wouldn't go near one, let alone set foot inside one, after the little boy's death. If she went into hospital, she reasoned, the same fate would surely befall her as befell her little brother on his last visit to that place.

An author-parent describes how his child developed a generalized fear of going out, following the 'departure' and subsequent death of her twin sister:

'The little twin sister soon developed a deep anxiety about going out for a walk and it took much comforting and patience before she could finally put her anxiety into words: "But you will bring me back again, won't you?" Her little twin, of course, had gone away with us to the hospital and would never come back again. If this hospital journey had happened once, how was this little girl to be sure it would not happen again? And how terribly dangerous it might seem to go out anywhere. Even when walks and going out had again become enjoyable and normal, there was a church near to our home with a large crucifix overlooking the road, and if for any reason we had to pass this "dying Jesus", this particular child would always hide her eyes and run fast to get by it. We could not doubt, in the middle of our difficulties, that this experience of the little sister's death was deeply disturbing to the security of the children, whose widest separation of ages was only sixteen months, and who had been so much together.'

Fears of this sort, which arise when a child identifies with his sibling, often revolve around talisman fantasies of a very primitive kind. Children believe they will die when they reach the age at which the sibling died, or else on the same day of the year or, perhaps, when certain external circumstances occur in conjunction as they did on the fateful day of his death. One or two children were reported to celebrate the anniversary of the death with an onset of psychosomatic 'symptoms' and one child who developed fairly severe asthma immediately after the death of his sister had recurring attacks every Christmas, which was the time of year she had died. It is worth pointing out of course that conditions such as asthma often occur seasonally in this way, without necessarily being sparked off by a psychological stimulus.

The sibling's fear of death and dying arises from a number of other sources as well as identifying with the dead child. For many children, fear arises directly from misconceptions about the nature of death and dying. We have already seen how inadequate parental explanations can give rise to grossly distorted ideas about death, but misconceptions and fantasies can also arise from what we as adults may think of as the 'harsh realities' of death itself.

If for a moment we try to look through the eyes of a young child we will realize that his confrontation with the so called 'realities' of death can be, and often is, nothing other than a 'fantasy' experience. Let me illustrate this point by reference to two cases I came across. In the first a young boy had a sister who was taken into hospital where she literally wasted away and died. Throughout the child's hospitalization the parents visited on a regular basis; every day the mother came she brought along her son as there was nobody to look after him at home. Throughout this period the boy witnessed his sister deteriorate both physically and mentally until she was no longer recognizable as the girl they once knew. Eventually even the features of her face began to change beyond recognition. Towards the end of this grisly ordeal the dying person (for whatever had happened to his sister, this was surely not her) no longer recognized either the boy or his mother and became totally unable to communicate with anyone. For the final few visits the transformed body lay under heavy sedation, though the doctor maintained that it was 'not quite over yet'. It took, in fact, quite a considerable time before it was declared that she'd died.

Perhaps one's first reaction on hearing of such a case is to retort that the boy should never have been exposed to such things and that someone was clearly to blame. This may well be true, although it is fashionable today to 'expose' children fully to death; my purpose here, however, is not to allocate blame or approval, but simply to draw attention to the quality of the brother's experience. Although at the time he showed remarkably little disturbance (at least, none was noticed by the people around him), it subsequently emerged that he had been very deeply disturbed by the episode.

What, after all, had he actually seen? The metamorphosis of his sister into a person who was not his sister but who was nevertheless still alive. It is hardly surprising that this confirmed in his mind the childish conception that even to be dead is still somehow to be alive. But what a fearsome and grotesque form of life it had proved to be. What, for example, could be meant by this death-person's refusal to speak to him or recognize him, he who was once her brother? What could it be but a punishment intended for him?

The fantasies aroused for this child by the 'reality' of death could fill many pages. What should be clear already is that in order to understand the child's reaction to an event such as this we must first understand what event he has actually perceived. In the present case it was not simply 'the death of his sister' that the little boy perceived. The very nature of death as a concept was defined for him by the cruel transformation he witnessed day after day in his sister's ward. At the end of this ordeal he was, in fact, more bewildered and more heavily burdened with fantasies about death than he was before it all started.

The ambiguity to a child of situations which are perhaps clear-cut to an adult is illustrated if anything more clearly in the second case. This case was similar to the last one in that the disabled child went from home to hospital where he was treated unsuccessfully and died. The sibling, another little boy who was seven-years-old was also taken to visit the dying child, though only once or twice. In hospital he found his brother reclining under piles of apparatus and was impressed by the presence of strange machines and masked doctors. After his brother's death the boy displayed an intense fear of doctors and hospitals and it emerged before long that on his visits to his brother he had perceived the doctors and nurses not in the role of life-savers but as actually being instrumental in his brother's death. One went into hospital so far as he had seen, not to be cured but in order for masked men to put one to death with their

112

fearsome machines. Once again, exposing the child to 'reality' in this way served only to frighten and confuse.

Most of the cases of fear I have looked at in this chapter are in some way related to the taboo on the subject of death. If parents and other involved parties were more ready to talk about death to the child and to introduce him positively to it when the time arose, the element of irrational fear would be considerably reduced.

Once again in this study, therefore, we find that it is incumbent on the parent to respond with thought and care for all of his children at a time when he is naturally preoccupied with a trauma which seems to be related to just one of them.

Realignment of the family

The parents' preoccupation with the deceased child can easily lead to a worse fate for the sibling than merely the suffering of temporary neglect. If parents do not quickly resolve the conflicts that have been generated for themselves by the death, they will in time inevitably promote a situation where their other children are unwittingly made to participate in these conflicts.

This can happen in a number of ways. Some parents were cited by caseworkers, for example, who, far from neglecting the siblings after the handicapped child's death, became suddenly overprotective of them. They lavished them with 'treats' and bowed to their every demand, but at the same time became extremely concerned with ensuring their absolute safety at all times. Such parents were clearly trying to make up to the sibling for past guilt-festered behaviour towards the handicapped child who had died. This sort of identification, or as one writer has called it 'mis-identification', of siblings by their parents was felt by some caseworkers to be quite common: they pointed to examples of children who had been explicitly conceived as substitutes for their dead brothers and sisters; one child was even reported to have been given the same name.

One social worker had been visiting a mother for a full two years after her handicapped child's death and even after this lapse of time the mother never wanted to talk about anything other than this child. She made consistently unfavourable comparisons between the dead child and the only other boy in the family such that it was as clear to the boy as to everyone else that she wished he and not his handicapped brother had died. Such a wish is indeed implicit in any case of identification like this. The memory of the dead child is kept alive at the expense of the individuality of his surviving sibling.

There are many aspects of a child's response to the death of a sibling that I have not touched on in this chapter. One important aspect that appeared in many families was quite simply a feeling of grief at the loss of a very close brother or sister. I have chosen not to concentrate here on a description of such grief for two reasons. Firstly, a great deal has already been written about the more 'ordinary' processes of grief and bereavement, and secondly, a simple grief reaction of this sort is not normally experienced by children under the age of about eleven. One important American study, for example, in which adults who had been bereaved in childhood were interviewed, found that when bereavement occurred under the age of nine not one of the subjects was able to recall any feelings of grief, although they remembered vividly other details of the death. It was only over the age of eleven that personal grief feelings were recalled (Furman 1970). For these reasons I have concentrated on the much less-researched subject of the younger child's response to a sibling's death. It goes without saying that older children are less plagued by the sort of fears and fantasies I have described, though, of course, they are just as likely to suffer from feelings of guilt along with their grief.

All children, regardless of age, tend to suffer after a sibling's death. If there is a single conclusion to be drawn from this chapter, it is that children tend to suffer in proportion to their parents ability both to cope with their own ambivalent feelings and to understand those of their children. The child of any age needs reassurance and support from his parents both on an emotional and on a conceptual level following the crisis of death. Young children need to be helped to understand what death actually is, older children require an atmosphere in which they can feel free to discuss openly their feelings of guilt and of loss. Only when the parents are alive to these needs and are not blinded by conflicts of their own can they realistically offer some help.

The death of a child will always be disturbing to the rest of its family. There is no way of guarding against this; no way of replacing what is lost, nor of eliminating the pain which this loss must inflict. What can be done, however, is to minimize the sources of a child's distress. If he cannot be sheltered from the tragedy of death, at least he can be spared the fantasy that he

114

himself is to blame, that hospitals are institutions for murder, or that death might reach down from heaven to take him away in the darkness of night.

References

Anthony, S. 'The Child's Discovery of Death'. Kegan Paul, London, 1940.

Cain, A., Fast, I. and Erikson, M. Children's disturbed reactions to the death of a sibling. 'American Journal of Orthopsychiatry', no. 34, 1964, p 741.

Challoner, L. 'How children think of death'. In 'Feeling and Perception in Young Children'. Tavistock Publications, London, 1963.

Cobb, B. Psychological impact of long illness and death on the family circle. 'J. Paediatrics', vol. 49, no. 6, 1956, pp 746-751.

Furman, R. The child's reaction to death in the family. In 'Loss and Grief, psychological management in medical practice', B. Schoenberg et al. (Eds). Columbia University Press, 1970.

Hilgard, J., Newman, M. and Fisk, F. Strength of adult ego following childhood bereavement. 'Amer. J. of Ortho-psychiatry', no. 30, 1960, p 788.

Koch, H. The relations of certain formal attributes of siblings to attitudes held towards each other and towards their parents. Monograph 78, Society for Research into Child Development, vol. 25, no. 4, 1960.

Marris, P. 'Widows and their Families'. London, 1958.

Nagy, M. The child's theory concerning death. 'J. Genet. Psychol'. no. 73, 1948, pp 3-26.

Orbach, C. The multiple meanings of the loss of a child. 'Amer. J. of Psychotherapy', vol. 13, no. 4, 1959, pp 906-915.

Veiga, M. Family reactions to the hospitalization of children with mental disorders. 'Amer. J. of Orthopsychiatry', no. 34, 1964, p 145.

Weston, D. and Irwin, R.   Pre-school child's response to death of infant sibling.   'Amer. J. of Diseases in Children', no. 106, 1963, p 564.

Wolff, S.   'Children Under Stress', Penguin, London, 1969.

9 Other fears and anxieties

In the last chapter I looked at some fairly complex forms of guilt which were aroused in siblings whose handicapped brother or sister had died. In this chapter I shall look at a number of other emotional reactions which may be thought of as potentially disturbing for the sibling.

Apart from those forms of guilt already considered there are many quite specific fears and anxieties which are likely to be present in siblings who grow up in families with a handicapped child. As with guilt, these emotions may only emerge as significant forces in the life of the child when external events take a decisive or a disruptive turn, for example on the death of the handicapped child or some other member of the family, after a serious marital row, following the loss of a boyfriend or girlfriend, or failure at school or work. At such times the sibling's irrational fears and anxieties, which have perhaps been dormant for some time, may suddenly appear to be rationally justified and will therefore be strongly reinforced.

1. FEARS ARISING FROM IDENTIFICATION

I have already pointed out that able-bodied children sometimes identify with their handicapped siblings in a disturbing way, perhaps even to the extent of developing imaginary 'handicaps' themselves. There is nothing inherently unusual about siblings identifying with one another, especially when they are relatively close in age. There are certain circumstances however, such as a handicapped child being put into permanent residential care, when the able-bodied sibling's identification with this child acts as a source of considerable anxiety for the sibling.

This was the case with Peter, a young boy who was extremely timid physically. He suffered from the age of ten from school refusal and an exaggerated fear of injuring himself. He wouldn't strike a match, he wouldn't learn to ride a bicycle let alone join in any of the rough-and-tumble games of his friends. His fears became so exaggerated that eventually he was referred to the child guidance clinic where it was discovered that Peter had a severely handicapped sister who had been put into residential care. Peter felt, not without some justification in view of the particular circumstances of this case, that his sister had not only been sent away physically but had also been rejected as a person from the life of the family. The child guidance clinic soon found out that Peter was frightened of injuring himself in case he too became 'handicapped' and like his sister had to be sent away.

Fear of this sort is not uncommon amongst siblings of children who have been put into care. More than one child I came across refused to go to school apparently as a direct result of such fears, the handicapped sibling having been 'sent away' to school, never to come home again.

Identification of course may not be the only element in the arousal of fear and anxiety in this connection. The mere fact that a brother or sister is being sent away can be a big disruption in the life of a child for a variety of reasons. The reaction of one young child is described in the following discussion by a social worker who was visiting the family in question during the period when they decided to put their handicapped child into care.

MB: This mother has only recently decided to let her child go into care. She was getting too big to handle and she used to get very bad chest infections and every so often would have to be rushed into hospital, so she decided to put her into care permanently and now has her home only at the weekends. The other toddler here was very upset about this, and indeed still is. She hasn't got through it yet, she gets up in the night and says 'Where' Janice? Janice doesn't have to go into hospital, she's our baby' and all this sort of thing. She gets into quite a state about it.

SK: Why do you think that is?

MB: Well they had been very close together, the mother had always given a lot of attention to Janice, the handicapped girl, and this little one was in on it in rather a protective role. The elder one was looked upon as her baby, so she would help to look after her and so on, and then of course she couldn't accept the idea that she was going to have to go away.

· Other fears and anxieties

SK: Do you think the mother herself accepted the idea?

MB: Oh no, not at all. This is what my visiting is very much about. The mother has had great difficulty about this, she's talked about it over and over again.

SK: And do you think her conflict has somehow rubbed off on to the younger child.

MB: Yes, yes, I am sure, she is a very good mother but she is very much emotionally tied up with the handicapped child. This mother does try very hard with the younger one, and she's very fond of her too. She'll get her special presents and give her treats when Janice is ill, but there have been problems definitely.

SK: Are these problems mainly a question of the sibling being anxious about Janice or do you see them mainly in terms of her relationship with her mother?

MB: I think in this case the sibling is generally anxious and confused. She cannot reconcile the idea that this is their baby with the fact that she had to be sent away, and what's made things worse here is that the mother has been in two minds as to whether or not she should have another child. She would like to and yet there's some chance that it might be handicapped. Every now and again the little one has heard about this and she'll say 'But Janice is our baby', and Janice is being pushed out as far as she's concerned. I think this new dilemma has heightened her anxiety a lot.

Whether or not this sibling's anxieties arise from identifying with her handicapped sister, Janice, is something of an academic point in this sort of case. The girl's anxiety seems to be a reflection of her mother's sense of loss and confusion. On an emotional level she finds it hard to accept Janice's sudden removal from the family, while conceptually she is thoroughly confused by the family's talk of having another baby. Clearly an event of this sort can represent a considerable disruption in the life of the sibling, particularly when the parents themselves are very uncertain about their decision to put the other child into care and when, as a result of their uncertainty, they fail to discuss with the sibling exactly what they are doing and why.

2. FEARS ARISING FROM THE PHYSICAL PRESENCE OF THE HANDICAPPED CHILD

Very few children appear to be repulsed by the physical appearance of their handicapped siblings, no matter how badly deformed they may be. Nevertheless the physical presence of such a child can definitely be a source of fear for the sibling. By and large most of the fears which arise in this connection are related to uncontrolled aggressive and hostile behaviour on the part of the handicapped child. Such behaviour may occur because the parents are unwilling to reprimand the child who is handicapped, or it may simply be an outcome of loss of control resulting from brain damage in the child itself. Whichever is the case it can be a nuisance and sometimes even a real danger to a younger brother or sister, and in these cases is a realistic source of fear for the sibling.

Fears arising from behaviour disorders and aggressiveness can be exaggerated or minimized by a number of factors. If the family live in a large house, for example, the sibling will be able to escape from interference with little difficulty, whereas in a small house or a flat any hyperactive behaviour on the part of the handicapped child will be more frustrating and intolerable for the sibling.

In a similar way the mobility of the disruptive handicapped child assumes considerable importance to the sibling who is continually having to avoid confrontation or interference. As one young girl said of her sister (who is both physically and mentally disabled) 'If Sandra was better on her feet we'd live in terror of her. As it is we clear out of her way when she starts being a nuisance.'

Insofar as this sort of problem does occur for the sibling, it will inevitably affect him socially as well as on a purely domestic level. In the Schonell and Watts survey, twenty per cent of the families interviewed reported some curtailment of the social activities of siblings and twenty-two per cent reported that the presence of a handicapped child at home had an adverse effect on the number of people invited into the house.

The reluctance of siblings to invite their friends home to play is in fact extremely common, and disruptive behaviour by the handicapped child is by no means the only reason for this. Many children, especially older ones, are acutely aware of the social stigma of having a brother or sister who is different from other children. The shame they feel on this account is noticeably a product of social forces rather than being a direct response to the disabled child himself. The sibling, especially if he is a self-conscious teenager, is worried that his relationship to a handicapped, possibly deformed, child will tarnish the image he is trying to promote amongst his peers.

One twelve-year-old girl I interviewed spent a long time telling me how ashamed she felt to tell her friends about Angela (her severely retarded sister). She commented that when they wanted to deride someone they always said 'You're mental' and whenever she heard anyone saying that she just wanted to hide. Like many other siblings she never brought her friends home and hoped they would never find out about Angela. Inevitably, though, two of them did and as she said, 'the whole class knows now and that's what they think of when they say "you're mental".'

What makes matters worse for many siblings in this predicament is that they find themselves in the awkward position of betraying their family in front of their friends. One fifteen-year-old girl said this:

'I really hate him (the handicapped brother) when he tries to join in with my friends and me. He always wants to join in and he spoils all our games so I don't ask my friends round now, I always go out to them. But sometimes I think: you are a cow. He can't help being like he is.'

A number of other writers have commented on the social embarrassment suffered by siblings of the handicapped. In America, Schreiber and Feeley started a discussion group for teenage siblings with the aim of drawing up a list of common problems facing these siblings. The following questions appeared high on the children's list:

a. How do you tell your friends about your retarded brother or sister, especially friends of the opposite sex?

b. How can we deal with our feelings when our friends show off their pictures of their siblings and talk about their accomplishments?

c. How do you deal with friends and people in school when you are hurt by their reference to the retarded as 'nutty' and 'crazy'?

The same questions were raised in a group for the siblings of brain-injured children run by R.F. Coleman in 1967. Coleman writes in his report:

'With regard to their own social life, the siblings frequently

121

found themselves unable to explain to their friends about their impaired brother or sister, they became embarrassed, angry and frustrated because they could not adequately cope with the situation socially or emotionally. In general they felt that the impaired child was a reflection on them and their family.'

Coleman concludes that:

'the findings from this group would indicate a need not only to educate the siblings with regard to brain injury but also to help them with their many emotional problems directly related to the impaired child, the home, and social situations.'

Coleman might have added here that the community itself is equally in need of education, for it should be remembered that the prejudice and derision for which the sibling feels himself to be a target has its origin outside his own family in the realms of the community as a whole - a fact well illustrated in the parents' letters published in the National Children's Bureau's book, 'Living with Handicap'. Some parents have pointed out for example that certain neighbours will not let their children play with a handicapped child especially if he is in some way mentally retarded. There may well be a conflict, therefore, between the child's own feelings about handicap and his desire to conform to the very different attitudes he will meet in the outside world - attitudes which are likely to be based on irrational fantasies as much as, if not more than, his own.

3. ANXIETIES ABOUT THE FUTURE

One of the other questions raised by Schreiber and Feeley's group was 'Does retardation lessen our chances of marriage and is it hereditary?' The two fears expressed in this question appear to be fairly widespread amongst siblings.

Siblings' anxieties about marriage and the problems of attracting a suitable partner may perhaps best be seen as an extension of the social anxieties examined above. Fears about their own capacity to produce healthy children, on the other hand, comprise a different sort of problem.

Unlike the somewhat diffuse anxiety related to social stigma, fears of this sort are more easily dealt with. Owing to advances in genetic research it is now known which disorders are likely to be carried forward to successive generations and what the chances of their being carried forward actually are. In any given case of, say, muscular dystrophy or mongolism, there may be uncertainty about the chances of a sibling's children being disabled, but for many conditions it is possible to say with certainty that there is no genetic basis for thinking that successive generations will be afflicted.

Of course the sibling may not know this and may in any event be too frightened to find out. One or two caseworkers cited examples of adult siblings who had definitely decided not to have children of their own, even though there was no genetic basis for assuming they would be disabled, for reasons which were explicitly related to their experience of handicap. Some caseworkers felt that the siblings' attitude to this corresponded in many families to the attitude of their parents. If, for example, the mother was worried about the chances of her children's offspring being handicapped, this anxiety, regardless of whether or not it was justified, was easily transmitted to the children themselves. In a similar way, when faced with difficult decisions about childbirth, certain siblings seemed most likely to adopt the same solution as their parents.

That there is sometimes a real cause for heartsearching as a result of genetic endowments is beyond doubt. In the extract which follows, a social worker describes a young girl facing a decision which few people could easily make.

DP: The boy himself is not expected to live beyond his late teens, and there is the added problem here that the able-bodied girl is also a carrier, but they are an incredible family in how they cope. Mrs Stokes is very relaxed and on my first visit told me all about it, and how she'd explained the genetic implications to Vera, the older girl.

SK: How did the older girl cope with this? It must have been a terrible blow to her to discover that she is probably carrying this disease and might pass it on to her own children in the future.

DP: They've carried out lots of tests, the chromosome change that causes muscular dystrophy can happen just at the moment of conception or it can be carried forward from the mother, so chromosome tests were done on the mother and Vera, and they told them that there was an 80 per cent chance, because this is the accuracy of the test, that the change had occurred when Chris was born and that Vera was therefore clear. Mrs Stokes told Vera this and she apparently replied 'Well, I think I'd rather adopt children anyway because it seems to be rather a messy business having them. ' This was at the age of 13; the fact that the mother has very successfully adopted a child herself makes Vera as an adolescent, feel that this is a satisfactory solution. Obviously she will have to think again, and terribly hard, when she gets older, but at the moment that is her solution.

There can be no doubt that some siblings do face enormous problems relating to childbirth. It would be interesting to know whether siblings' own families are in fact smaller than average as a result of these problems. It is perhaps worth noting in this respect that in a national survey conducted by Crew in 1959, 90 per cent of mothers thought that the best family size consisted of two or more children. In contrast to this Holt looked at a sample of mothers who had a retarded child and found that even in the most favourable group of mothers, whose first child was retarded, 60 per cent did not want another child. It is true that for many of these mothers their decision might have been only a short-lived reaction, but it is beyond doubt that an unfavourable attitude to childbirth did exist in this group as a whole and it is not unreasonable to speculate that such an attitude could well affect the attitudes of the next generation. Clearly, though, this is a question that only careful research can answer.

4. INEXPLICABLE ANXIETY

What other sources of fear and anxiety are there for the siblings living in the sort of family I have described. The ones I have looked at so far - the fear of being sent away like the handicapped child, the fear of having children oneself, anxieties arising about what other people will think or say - all of these are specific in so far as each one has a referent which is clearly identifiable. However, there is another sort of anxiety facing the sibling which is less tangible than any of these and whose referent is not easily named. The nature of this 'inexplicable anxiety' was illustrated many years ago by Dr H.C. Cameron who drew a comparison between the behaviour of very young children and that of birds under stress. Chicks and fledglings can be handled, photographed and fed without showing any signs of being upset or disturbed, provided the mother bird is far away. If, however, she is nearby her own agitation is communicated to the brood with the utmost rapidity. In the same way even the most loving mother will communicate something of her own personal irrational anxieties

to her small children, though the children may be quite unaware
of the source of anxiety.

In this way the fears and worries of parents which were
outlined in chapters four and five and also what Olshansky called
the 'pervasive sorrow' attendant on the birth of a handicapped
child may unavoidably be transmitted within the family.

It is hard to illustrate anxiety of this sort simply because it
is non-specific and infectious in nature, but it seems to appear
most often in families where parents have tried to conceal their
own worries from their children or where they find the reality
of a situation too painful to discuss or even think about.

In one such family the sibling had a sister who was perfectly
healthy until she was three years old. At this age she was
suddenly taken ill and whisked into hospital; when she returned
she was totally disabled both physically and mentally. Her little
brother found this very hard to understand and was full of anxious
questions. Would Caroline ever walk again? Would she ever
talk? Would she be going to school? The parents were deeply
shocked by what had happened, so much so that they were unable
to face the truth about the little girl's future and were therefore
unable to answer the boy's questions. He in turn could see that
something disastrous had happened, furthermore, he could sense
the disaster in his parents' reactions. The more his questions
were avoided and fobbed off, therefore, the more the parents'
anxiety was transmitted to him.

It can be extremely hard for parents to cope with a child's
questions at a time like this when they can scarcely cope with
their own emotions. It is understandable, therefore, especially
in view of the fact that no parent wishes to expose his child to
unnecessary emotional upheaval, that the sibling is often 'sheltered' from the truth. Paradoxically, of course, the desire of
parents to protect their children from painful realities is likely
to cause more pain and worry in the long run than the child would
otherwise suffer. For many of the families where this was happening, caseworkers were quick to point out that although open
discussion was nominally suppressed 'in the interests of the children', in reality it was all too clearly suppressed as a result of the
parents' own defences against the truth. One could say a great
deal more about general or 'non-specific' anxiety amongst siblings.
The high level of anxiety amongst the children was illustrated by
the frequency with which caseworkers reported enuresis, school
refusal, clinging and other associated signs, though it should be

remembered that these are not always signs of anxiety, but may be developmental disorders. Some psychoanalytically orientated psychiatrists such as Pearson (1949) describe anxiety as arising from the child's fear of instinctively expressing his aggression, whilst others such as Sullivan (1947) write of the anxiety induced by his awareness of dependance. These two viewpoints have particular relevance to our understanding of siblings in view of the evidence presented in chapters seven and eight respectively.

Learning theorists on the other hand tend to view anxiety as a fear of anticipated punishment, in the widest sense of that word. They point out that this fear often can arise from a conflict of interests, for example when the child's desire to secure the approval of his friends is in conflict with his desire to secure the approval of his family. When this happens one of these two motivating forces must partially succumb to the other, leading inevitably to the disapproval of either his peers or his family, which is in this case the 'punishment' he fears. Theoretical insights of this sort have a great deal to offer the social worker or parent who is trying to allay the sibling's anxieties and dispel his fears. Of the 'rational fears' that siblings experience many can at least be partially guarded against. The aggressive child with brain injury can perhaps be restrained or his sibling given a key to his own room; doubts about being a carrier of the disease can be settled through genetic counselling; fantasies about disability can be removed with accurate up-to-date information, and so on. Fears which have less rational foundations may also be dispelled if the child feels sufficiently secure with the adults around him to express them. For the rest we should remember that in order to dispel the anxiety of the child it may be necessary first to dispel the anxiety of his parents, and beyond that to attack that prejudice in society as a whole which has caused the handicapped and their families to carry in the first place the unnecessary burden of a social stigma.

References

Adams, M. 'The Mentally Subnormal: The Social Casework Approach'. Heinemann, London, 1960.

Cameron, H.C. 'The Nervous Child'. Oxford Medical Publications, London, 1918.

Coleman, R.F. 'Group work with brain injured children and their siblings'. 4th Annual Conference of the Association for Children with Learning Disabilities. New York, 1967.

Holt, K. The influence of a retarded child upon family limitation. 'J. of Ment. Def. Research', vol. 2, part 1, June 1958.

Pearson, G.R. 'Emotional Disorders of Childhood'. Norton, New York, 1949.

Pikunas, - and Clary, - Fears in normal and emotionally disturbed children. 'J. of Psycholog. Studies'. no 13, 1962, pp 157-164.

Schonell, F.J. and Watts, B.H. A first survey on the effects of a subnormal child on the family unit. 'Amer. J. of Ment. Def.' no. 61, 1957, p 210.

Schreiber, M. and Feeley, M. Siblings of the retarded: a guided group experience. In 'Management of the Family of the Mentally Retarded', Wolfensberger, W. and Kurtz, R.A. (Eds). Follett Educational Corporation, USA, 1969.

Sullivan, H.S. 'Conceptions of Modern Psychiatry'. Norton, Washington, 1947.

Younghusband, E., et al. 'Living with Handicap'. National Children's Bureau, London, 1970.

10   Obstacles to normal growth

'Because handicaps are long-term problems, they can affect
the overall emotional growth and development of the other
children in the household.'

E. Poznanski.

It is not so long ago in terms of the history of ideas that children
were regarded as miniature adults and the child's growth towards
maturity was seen simply as a process of 'getting bigger' in mind
and body. Today, of course, we view childhood in a very different
way from this. At about the turn of the last century psychologists
began to grow aware of the fact that children are essentially different in nature as well as in size from the adults they later become. Indeed, since then a whole new science has grown up
around the study of childhood growth and development.

Developmental psychology has stressed from its inception
that the child cannot usefully be regarded as a little adult, for in
doing this we lose sight of the psychological nature of those transformations which children go through in their journey towards
maturity. These transformations are marked by differences in
the quality of experience and understanding as well as in more
quantitative aspects of development. This point was illustrated
in an earlier chapter when we saw that the nature of a child's
understanding of death is very much a product of his age.

It is the job of the developmental psychologist to understand
the processes involved in each stage of development and thus to
explain the hows and whys that lie behind them. One of the first
insights that developmental psychologists hit upon was that a
child's growth can be arrested or fixated at any of the crucial
stages it normally passes through. The arrest of development
need not affect the whole child; on the contrary, children who
have failed to develop fully in some particular dimension may
grow up to be otherwise fully mature individuals.

128

There is a theory that these arrests or fixations are frequently caused by some form of emotional trauma in childhood
and proponents of this theory are generally agreed that development cannot continue in the area in question, no matter how far
advanced the person may be in other areas of his life, until the
conflict or trauma responsible for the arrest has been fully
resolved.

What has all this got to do with siblings of the disabled?
The answer at present can only take the form of another question.
Do the stressful experiences of the siblings I have described in
any way prevent the full emotional and social development of
these children? And if so, how?

I should point out straight away that I myself have not set out
to answer this question systematically, and it is highly doubtful
whether the unstructured observations of family caseworkers can
go any real way towards solving it.

Most of the reactions I have looked at in this book have been
on the level of emotions, feelings and patterns of individual and
family behaviour which are essentially immediate and therefore
short-term reactions to crisis. Despite this, however, it is
perhaps not out of place in a book such as this to offer some
thoughts on the long-term effects on siblings, even though there
are only the roughest of clues to work from. For although the
presence of any detrimental long-term effects on siblings is only
an assumption on our part until we have conducted observations
of a more controlled nature, the presence of many enduring
problems, upon which this assumption is based, can hardly be
disputed. Without entering into undue speculation, therefore, let
us examine those problems of an enduring nature encountered by
siblings, which are most likely to be associated with developmental arrest in some sphere of their life.

There are many possible long-term problems for siblings,
but by and large they fall into two quite distinct clusters. On the
one hand are those arising in families who react to handicap by
strongly rejecting their handicapped child, either by excluding
him altogether from the family group or else by keeping him
within the family but treating him overtly or implicitly with
hostility and resentment. Parents in this group are likely to look
to the able-bodied siblings to compensate in some way for the
deficiencies of the handicapped child. The siblings therefore
tend to be overprotected, encouraged to excel or treated as high-
class china in an effort to ensure that they are perfect and remain
so.

129

The other cluster of problems arises in families who react in the opposite way, that is by bowing to every demand of the handicapped child and placing him in the very centre of family life. In families where this happens the siblings face a very different sort of problem. Here they tend to be pushed into the background and neglected as individuals and very often they are used more as au pairs and home-helps than brothers and sisters by parents whose chief aim seems to be the indulgence of their handicapped child.

It was pointed out earlier in the book that these two apparently opposite reactions are really only opposite poles of a single dimension, and for this reason are closely related forms of response. The parent who so eagerly over-indulges his handicapped child is covering up strong negative feelings at some level of consciousness and many parents visibly waver from one response to another. Similar though the origin of such responses may be, however, they are completely dissimiliar in terms of their effects and therefore we should perhaps distinguish the two groups in terms of the problems that siblings face rather than in terms of the parental attitude to handicap itself.

In the first group, then, it was noticed by caseworkers that certain siblings seemed to be expected to compensate for a handicapped child who was perceived predominantly as a source of disappointment and a mark of personal failure. One eight-year old girl, Judith Stimpson, was described by a caseworker in the following way:

> 'She's a very precious little girl trying to do ever so well. She's only a little thing and she'll come in and it's quite obvious that she most desperately wants your approval. I'm sure unconsciously the mother realizes that Justin (a four-year-old with spina bifida) won't make it, so she pushes it all on to Judith and Judith is meant to be so perfect. I have to be shown how well Judith reads and how well she does this and that. She's just a very precious little doll who performs, that's the best way I can put it; she's really a very weird kid, not at all like a normal eight-year-old.'

The same caseworker remarked on this doll-like quality in other siblings. Of Martha Wright she says:

> 'Martha is also like Judith Stimpson; she's a very precious little thing and she has to do everything ever so well. She has to make out all the time that she's a good little girl. Even

when she sits down she does it so neatly and tidies her dress;
you notice at once there's something wrong; it's really weird
to see.

SK: Do you know what she's like at school?

JB: I think she's a very model little girl at school, but that
seems to happen with a lot of these kids, especially the little
girls. They are very good in school. They are such good little
girls that perceptive headmistresses realize there's something
wrong and complain about it. I got this with Monica Bathurst.
The headmistress is worried about Monica because Monica is
so good, she doesn't behave like a little girl. Like Judith
Stimpson and Martha Wright they are too good. I know it
sounds crazy but it's a sign of disturbance when they are like
that; it may not be gross but none-the-less they're growing
up in a very affected way.'

The same sort of picture was painted by nearly all of the caseworkers for at least some of their cases. The pressures on one
adolescent boy to compensate for his handicapped sister were
described as follows:

'The older boy has been made to achieve or has been made to
try to achieve great things, which in fact he hasn't been doing.
His sister is very handicapped. She's resident in Queen Mary's.
Her prognosis is very poor; in fact she's more or less a
vegetable really. The parents quite blatantly expect David to
make up for this by excelling. They got him into a grammar
school and he was pushed considerably, but after starting well
in his first year he went steadily downhill and only got one 'O'
level eventually; he's now left school and has had four jobs in
eight months. He talks to me a lot and says he's very unhappy.
I think the pressure on him to achieve has been quite enormous.'

In another family a caseworker describes how the initial need of
the parents to have a child who excelled lost much of its strength
only after they had given birth to two other perfectly able-bodied
children.

'Dad was a junior surgical registrar; he's just had promotion,
now he's a senior registrar. They are a mixed marriage, the
mother is English and they both had the feeling at first that
this defective child was somehow an inevitable product of their
mixed marriage. I remember the father saying "he's the sort

of child you might expect to be born of a mixed marriage. "
He obviously knew better from a medical point of view, but he
was worried that that's what people would think. There's no
doubt that this child's deformity brought to the surface some
very delicate feelings about colour and marriage that the
parents had never before dared to discuss. Anyway they had
another child, Pauline, who was okay and they really made
her fulfil their need for an attractive achieving child. They
put a great deal of pressure on her to be..... well - perfect.
But since then they've had the other two and Pauline's grown
up a bit, they're beginning to develop their self-esteem on
all fronts and there's not nearly so much pressure on Pauline,
she's much more taken for granted. '

In all of these cases there is a similar need to excel. A need
which appears to be imposed initially by the parents on the able-
bodied siblings in order to compensate for the shortcomings
(whether imagined or real) of the handicapped child. A need,
moreover, which is often internalized by the siblings so that they
feel themselves that they must excel in order to live up to their
parents' expectations. In the case of David, and as in all of
these cases to some extent, since no child can ever attain such
a state of perfection, his parents inevitably made him extremely
unhappy. Only when the parents adopt a more realistic attitude
by looking to these children for the qualities they actually possess
instead of looking for some general token of perfection, will
they be free to live happily and to develop fully into the unique
individuals they really are.

The second group of long-term problems I have described
seem to occur when the handicapped child assumes a central over-
indulged position in the family group. In this situation the siblings
are often used in the role of helpers in a way which severely
restricts their own social and intellectual life. The following
family situation was not unusual:

SK: You say the parents put extra responsibilities on to the
ten-year-old girl?

VE: Yes I think they do.

SK: What sort of expectations do they have of her vis a vis
the handicapped child which you think are not appropriate for a
girl of her age?

VE: Betty comes home at weekends and it annoys the parents immensely if Vicky wants to go out to play instead of remaining the whole time with Betty. They get very annoyed at this and often just won't let her go out. They expect her to be far more grown up and far less demanding than is reasonable for a girl of her age. In fact they expect her to behave rather like a grown up nurse to Betty whereas in reality she's only a little girl of ten.

The image of the sibling as a semi-professional helper is one that occurred to many caseworkers.

SK: Does she try to use the other brothers and sisters to look after the handicapped child?

WK: Yes. In fact she's almost employing the two nearest in age to the handicapped girl to look after her. Except, of course, they don't get paid.

And from another caseworker:

JB: Joseph is fifteen and about to leave school. He wants to work in a stable and become a jockey. They won't let him because he's the baby-sitter. When he comes home from school the mother is able to do her shopping and in the evening they are able to go out while he looks after Brian. Once they realized that if he became a jockey and worked in a stable he would have to leave home, they wouldn't let him carry on with that idea; they suggested he should get a job in the local post office instead.

And of another family:

JB: The father and mother adore Christine who is spastic and the whole family tends to revolve around Christine.

SK: In what way?

JB: You know, everything for Christine, she's got to be taken out everywhere. If Sue wants to go out swimming, she has to take Christine. If Sue wants to go to the park she has to take Christine. Sue has told me she feels that too much is put upon her; after all she is only twelve and they treat her sometimes like a registered child-minder.

These sorts of problems facing siblings may not constitute emotional traumas which lead to fixation. Indeed many of them seem to be quite 'normal' parent-child conflicts. But on the other hand they can, and often do, represent a very deep-seated source of conflict for the child. Many of these children are constrained by their parents to act in a way which is often inappropriate to their age; this can only lead to unhappiness for them. Furthermore they often do not have sufficient time to themselves to be able to engage in play and those rudimentary social activities which are known to be essential if the child is ever to grow into a full and mature individual.

This raises a further point which emerged very vividly in a number of case discussions. Many siblings are in effect deprived of a normal sibling relationship with their handicapped brother or sister, either because they are not allowed to have such a relationship, or else because they are unable to have one by the very nature of the handicap. Not a lot of research has been conducted in the field of normal sibling relationships but the little that has been done shows that the relationship of one child to another in a family performs a number of important functions in terms of the social development of each child. (Sutton-Smith and Rosenberg 1970). It is not hard to see, for example, how such basic social concepts as sharing, helping one another and being responsible for and responsible to other people, are learnt in a sibling relationship. It is perfectly true that they may be learnt in other sorts of relationship too, but in a society where the community seems to play an ever-diminishing role in the support and upbringing of a child, the sibling relationship is an increasingly important factor in the socialization of children in these ways.

Needless to say, many only children grow up without ever experiencing a sibling relationship and they do not appear to suffer because of this. But siblings of the handicapped, especially when the handicap in question is mental rather than physical, are often not merely deprived of a normal sibling relationship but are engaged in a sibling relationship that actually holds them back.

This can happen in a fairly mild way by the sibling simply being grouped together with the handicapped child, a fate which seems to befall many siblings. Comments such as the following, which come from three different caseworkers, are typical in this respect:

'All the case records are full of attempts to persuade mum to let Bernadette grow up. She was still trying to get her to go to bed at six o'clock with Rebecca when she was twelve-years-old. Rebecca has a mental age of five or six so Bernadette was being treated as an equal with a child who was not two years younger but about seven years younger, in terms of her real age.'

'The eight-year-old girl was treated very much like a baby, she was grouped together with her six-year-old sister and this other girl was very severely retarded and really was in effect a baby. The effect of this was only temporary and really only a phase that the family went through. It was something that I realized straight away and was able to talk to the mother about.'

'For example the two children had to go to bed together and come in from play at the same time. The parents always treated them the same in this way without ever realizing the resentment this was causing.'

In all of these cases the able-bodied siblings were older than their retarded brothers and sisters and were therefore being treated as very considerably younger than their real age. When the converse occurs, although the sibling is initially treated as older than his real age, this imputed age will increasingly become younger as the years go by for he will gradually overtake the retarded child in both ability and intelligence.

On the whole it is unlikely that this sort of problem alone has any really serious or lasting effect on the growth and development of the sibling. Perhaps more serious than this is the sort of generic communication problem that sometimes arises in families with a child who has speech or language difficulties. In one such family the parents developed an elementary sign language for the benefit of their little boy who was deaf. They began to use this language so much that even when the deaf boy was not around they continued to communicate in predominantly non-verbal ways. The boy's younger sister was therefore born into a family in which there was a very restricted use of speech and her own speech simply failed to develop. For a time it was thought that she too might be defective in some way until it was established that there was no physical or mental reason for her lack of speech. The reason was social. She had neither been talked to nor expected to reply through the medium of words but rather through the medium of signs and signals. As a result, this extraordinary pattern of communication, which had been developed in deference to the needs of the deaf boy, had left its mark on the little girl's linguistic development.

Another family had an eldest child who was both deaf and

dumb. Each of the three brothers and sisters who followed him was physically sound but fell into the pattern of withdrawn non-communicating children who were extremely backward in linguistic and verbal skills. Here the mother, who assumed sole responsibility for the care of the children, had become so distressed at her failure to make her first child understand what she wanted to say that she virtually gave up trying to communicate with him at all. This pattern, once established, seemed to be carried over in a way that affected all the successive children. In a household which was starved of speech it was little wonder that they ended up in the way that they did, backward and socially disadvantaged in this respect.

For obvious reasons there is some danger of a basically intelligent child being held back intellectually if he patterns himself too closely on a severely or even only a mildly retarded sibling. This in fact was one of the conclusions of J.C. Coleman following his experimental group sessions with parents of mentally deficient children. His groups were attended by approximately one third of the parents of retarded children at a special school. One of the three basic problems for siblings that these parents raised was that 'They tended to suffer "intellectually" by having to play and interact with a retarded child.' There is doubtless some truth in this but also significant is the fact that the emotional upheaval wrought by handicap in the lives of these children will detract from the time and effort they put into study and schoolwork. Careful research into the effect of handicap on the school attainment and attendance of siblings has not yet, to my knowledge, been done, but would surely prove well worthwhile.

In this chapter I have shown that because of the presence of a handicapped child, siblings are often expected to behave in ways that are not appropriate to their age and abilities. I have looked at some of those circumstances surrounding handicaps of different kinds that are conducive to a slower development by siblings in certain aspects of their growth than they might otherwise expect. We have seen that many children miss out on important aspects of childhood because they are either expected to be perfect children in compensation for their handicapped brothers and sisters or else they are expected to act like adults taking on a child-minding role towards these siblings. We have seen that as a result of all this children can be backward in their development of speech and language and in other educational spheres. I have suggested also that those children who are not

able or allowed to have a normal brother or sister relationship
in terms of their play and general interaction, are likely to suffer
socially. Many children are not allowed to fight, play, make a
noise, express their anger, or indeed their joy, whenever their
handicapped sibling is near in case they upset or harm him in
some way. It is most unlikely that children can grow up in such
a restrictive atmosphere without their peer relationships, their
social attitudes and to some extent their own personalities being
affected. When a child is retarded, older siblings tend to be
held back in their development and younger siblings lack that
spur to develop which a normal sibling would provide (Farber
1968). I have not dealt in this chapter with the impact of handicap on a sibling's emotional development since this has been dealt
with implicitly in earlier chapters. All of the emotional conflicts or fears and anxieties that I have described elsewhere can
of course persist for a very long period of time, and when this
happens the child's emotional growth will rarely remain unscarred.

As I said at the beginning of this chapter, the long-term
effects of events on people are hard to calculate exactly. Indeed,
the effects on individual persons cannot be calculated at all
except by making an informed guess, that is by comparing the
individual's development with the developmental norms of a
specially selected control group. Clearly I have not done this in
the present case. But there is, nevertheless, some evidence to
suggest that handicap can act as a barrier to a child's full and
healthy development. Sufficient evidence, at least, to alert us in
our professional and parental roles to the danger of ignoring
this possibility, and perhaps failing to notice the distorting
effect on the life of the sibling.

References

Farber, B. 'Mental Retardation - It's Social Context and Social
    Consequences'.   New York, 1968.

Poznanski, E. Psychiatric difficulties in siblings of handicapped
    children. 'Clinical Paediatrics', vol. 8, no. 4, 1969.

Sutton-Smith, B. and Rosenberg, B.G. 'The Sibling'. HRW,
    USA, 1970.

11 The children who cope

One caseworker commented on her caseload as follows:

'To my surprise I have found very little real disturbance due to the handicap of a sibling'

another said:

'In general, I was surprised that the siblings on my caseload did not show a greater degree of disturbance'

Although these were the only two comments of their sort from caseworkers, it should be clear that a very large number of siblings are not greatly affected by the presence of a handicapped child in their family. How is it that these children are well adjusted and able to cope with the difficult situations I have described, whereas others are clearly unable to do so?

There are many possible criteria for good adjustment and the ability to cope. In assessing any particular child on a variety of criteria we might find that he fails in social relationships and competence, for example, but passes in self attitudes, self realization and perception of reality. Can we in these circumstances say that he is well adjusted? There is no clear answer to this question because there is no self evident way of deciding which criteria are of greater importance. As one psychiatrist put it 'there are many ways to be adjusted and to lead a reasonably happy and productive life. One mode of adjustment might meet some criteria, and another mode, other criteria' (Buss, 1966).

This is virtually the same problem as we faced in chapter 3. If there is no clear way of deciding whether or not a child is disturbed, there can also be no clear way of deciding whether or not he is coping and well adjusted.

Once again, however, there clearly is a pragmatic value in making a distinction of just this sort, for despite the difficulties of assessment it is important that we know how some siblings are able to avoid the sort of crises I have been talking about, and how others, although unable to avoid them, are at least able to resolve them satisfactorily.

In chapter 3 I pointed out that many aspects of a sibling's reaction to having a handicapped brother or sister, although disturbing to the child himself, were, given the circumstances, not necessarily abnormal or even undesirable. A certain amount of anxiety and fear, for example, and a shared sense of family disaster are only to be expected from any child over the age of about four or five when he finds himself in the middle of the trauma that the birth of a severely handicapped child can represent in the life of his family.

Because such disturbed reactions may be regarded as either 'normal' or 'abnormal', depending on our point of view, the problem of how we should decide whether a child is coping satisfactorily or failing to do so, is even more difficult.

One can only rely on a rule of thumb, and for my present purposes I shall hold that the child is coping well who, despite the problems and strains which he faces, is somehow able to reorganize his life in a way which minimizes the effect of any stress. Coping, in this sense, is not a question of being without problems and difficulties but is rather a matter of organizing one's external life and also one's internal resources in such a way that these problems can be overcome and do not constantly interfere with other areas of life. In terms of the concept of crisis, the coping child is one who is able to regain the equilibrium which has been temporarily upset by the crisis situation.

How, then, can this equilibrium be restored? We have already seen that there are many ways in which it may be upset; correspondingly there are many ways in which it may be safeguarded or restored.

MITIGATION OF THE EFFECTS OF HANDICAP

Crises that are caused by disability may be solved when disability itself is avoided or overcome. Some children, for example, are only handicapped temporarily, their conditions being easily corrected by surgery or the passage of time. A bilateral cleft palate is a defect which can be very disturbing to see in a new born baby, but which becomes virtually unnoticeable after surgery. In this sort of case there is every chance that any disturbed equilibrium in the life of the sibling, or in the rest of the family, will be quickly restored without any need for major reorganizations. One caseworker talked of the 'ascending spiral' in families where the condition of the handicapped child underwent gradual improvement.

The effect of handicaps which are more enduring in nature can also often be mitigated. In one family a five-year-old girl had cerebral palsy and although she was a reasonably intelligent little girl she was unable to get her wishes across to her parents because they couldn't understand her speech. She became extremely frustrated as a result of this and reacted by being very naughty and aggressive. The mother especially became very overwrought because she felt she had worked so hard with Tina, the handicapped girl, and yet despite all her efforts seemed to be 'landed' with a very naughty child who was a continual nuisance to her. Naturally this situation affected the whole family group and for a time there seemed to be little hope of relief. However, Tina was eventually offered special classes in speech therapy which she herself proved extremely keen to have. Gradually her speech began to improve and as Tina was able to communicate more successfully, so a primary source of frustration in the family was removed. Once again the caseworker noticed an ascending spiral in the family as a whole.

When a handicap can be overcome in this way one might justifiably argue that it was not in the first place very severe. A large part of Tina's disability, after all, was quite literally removed. How do families and siblings cope when the disabled child is suffering from a condition which cannot be rectified in such a practical way?

PARENTAL ADJUSTMENT

Perhaps the most important single factor in the adjustment of siblings is the adjustment of parents themselves. This point was raised by nearly every single caseworker both in general discussion and in relation to particular case studies. The following comments are taken from caseworkers' replies to section C of the questionnaire.

'A lot depends on the stability of the marriage and the intelligence and understanding of the mother.'

· The children who cope

'The emotional acceptance of the handicap by the parents is of great value, as it gives siblings confidence and stability.'

'In the more stable marital relationships the siblings do appear to have fewer problems.'

'If family communications improve everything else seems to as well .... marital problems and difficulties form a large part of the disturbances showing in the handicapped child and his siblings.'

'Where disturbance (of a sibling) has been present in any degree it can usually be attributed to the parents' handling of the situation.'

Of one particular case a worker said:

'This is an easy one, it's the sort of family with a handicapped child one would love to see more of, and this comes back to what I feel generally about this. That if the family and the parents especially have a mature relationship, then they cope with the handicapped child and are able to adjust as a family to any difficulties they meet. This is a very nice family situation, two very happy people married to each other, and you can feel this as soon as you go into their home. The elder girl who is not handicapped is a delightful little girl who seems to accept the handicap of her brother very well without being unduly affected by it. The boy is quite a bad spina bifida and probably a bit retarded. In spite of the fact that he's been in hospital a great deal, the family support him in a very sensible way without doting on him, and he himself is very little disturbed. The parents treat him just as normally as they possibly can. For example his sister had a big birthday party and when his birthday came he said could he have a party, and they said yes, and could he have who he wanted, and they said yes. So he invited half his form and they had a party for seven handicapped children and they didn't turn a hair. I heard tapes of the party and it was obviously a great success. Everyone enjoyed it. If all families were like this, I think we'd be out of a job. Mind you, having said that, I think that this is a very important part of our work because the mother here talks to me very fully about what she feels and really does use me. She seems to get rid of a lot of anxieties by using me. I think she'd manage without us, but I think she does just a little better by having someone to talk to specifically about this. On the

whole then no problems or disturbances for the sibling with
the handicap here at all, and I think it's the family situation
that this comes back to.'

This sort of conclusion on the part of caseworkers has been
endorsed by a number of writers. Michael Begab claims that if
there are disturbances in siblings of the handicapped these
'normally coincide with disturbances in their parents'. Graliker,
Fishler and Koch, in a study of the families of mentally retarded
children found that sibling reactions were related to parents'
reactions to the abnormal child; in cases where the retarded
child was accepted by the parents, older siblings showed no disturbance at home or school or in their social activities. Ann
Gath, after a study of the siblings of children with Down's
Syndrome, says :

'Graliker, Fishler and Koch (1932) reported that siblings are
affected by the attitude of the parents to the handicapped child.
Certainly in the present study disturbance was reported in
siblings whose parents expected them to overcompensate for
the disappointment of a handicapped child.'

Schreiber and Feeley also stressed the importance of good communication and feeling between parents and adolescent siblings
of the handicapped. And there is no doubt that this applies to
children of all ages. Good communication, they claimed,
depends on the existence of the kind of relationship which encour-
ages the adolescent to go to his parents whenever he feels the
need.

There are clearly a number of specific ways in which
parents can help siblings. Open sensitive communication about
delicate subjects - such as the long-term meaning of handicap,
institutionalization or death - is undoubtedly important for the
sibling's understanding and acceptance of the situation. A little
parental insight into the restructuring (if there has been any) of
family roles and organization as a result of handicap can also go
a long way. Many families were cited in which mild sibling problems and mild signs of disturbance disappeared altogether when
parents realized that the siblings in question were somehow
missing out on affection and attention. Some slight but meaningful readjustment on their part was usually enough to reassure
them. The following report is typical :

· The children who cope

'The eldest girl here was very good with the handicapped girl
when she was young. She was very helpful with Helen who is
the handicapped one. She'd always run and fetch the powder
and this sort of thing, she was always keen to do things for her,
though I'm sure, in fact, that she was very jealous of Helen.
Then when she went to school she didn't settle well at all, she
wouldn't have school dinners, she had to have sandwiches
apparently so that she could follow the school helper around.
She never played with the other children. Lots of little things
like that built up and went on for a long time. The mother
eventually grew very conscious about these problems and she
began to feel that Joyce had missed out because Helen had
come so soon after her and then there'd been another child
after that. The mother felt that she had neglected the eldest.
As a result of this she started spending much more time with
her and deliberately making an effort with her, and Joyce's
problems almost immediately started to resolve themselves.'

The parents' capacity to remain relatively stable whilst in the
middle of minor or even major changes and adjustments of life-
style seems to be a crucial element if the equilibrium of the
whole family is ever to be retained. But how can parents cope
with the 'secondary' sources of problems within the family, such
as the problems of their able-bodied children, indeed how can
they adjust to, and meet, the needs of any of their children if
they are preoccupied with their own inadequacy or distress?

Parents from different families are able to maintain their
stability in differing ways and to varying degrees. They have a
variety of crisis-meeting resources. But by and large equilibrium seems most likely to be maintained within the family as a
whole, regardless of the amount of adjustments its various members need to make and the amount of personal distress they
endure, if the following criteria are fulfilled: that the handicap
itself is defined by the family in a realistic way and the true
nature of their crisis is understood; that they allow each other,
and are able themselves, to communicate freely about their
reactions, both positive and negative, to what has happened;
that they make decisions concerning readjustments to their
crisis jointly, and do not harbour separate and conflicting solutions; that they make readjustments and reorganizations in a
way which takes into consideration the needs of all family members, rather than the needs of just one or two.

We have already seen that the roles of both parents and children undergo a change as the life-cycle of any family unfolds. There is no doubt that people can adapt to quite major changes in their lives if they have to, and this is a capacity which parents need more than most in a family with a handicapped child. The difficulties come when the changes demanded of them are on the one hand too sudden and overwhelming, inviting hasty and excessive reactions which are detrimental to the family as a whole or, on the other hand, when parents are unable either to accept the child's handicap or to make any concessions to it at all, in which case fears and anxieties are suppressed and the needs of the family as a whole are once again thwarted. Between the Scylla and Charybdis of these two extremes lies the course that parents undoubtedly must seek if they wish to safeguard the health and welfare of their family.

OTHER FACTORS AFFECTING THE ADJUSTMENT OF SIBLINGS

1. Nature and degree of handicap

What other factors exist which affect the sibling's ability to adjust and cope?

The nature and degree of a child's handicap is one factor that has such an effect. Throughout this study I have treated all sorts of handicap, whether mental or physical, minimal or severe, as essentially the same. This is because these distinctions have little bearing on the structure of parental or sibling response. Sheila Hewett confirms this when she says 'far more difficulties are shared by all families with a handicapped child than are specific to any medical category of handicap'. Having made this point, however, it should be quite clear that minimal handicaps are less likely to have a serious impact on a family than severe ones are, if only because it is easier for parents to treat the handicapped child as they would treat any normal child. This was a reason given by many caseworkers for the absence of problems for certain siblings.

SK: How have they managed to cope as a family?

GL: Extremely well. This is a very stable family. Mother hasn't got very good health at all but again there is a granny in the picture who helps a lot and the father does his bit. This is a good solid working-class family.

SK: And how have they adjusted themselves to having this handicapped child in the middle?

GL: Well he's not as handicapped as his brother was (he died) so they haven't needed any great adjustments. But I think they have coped extremely well. They always strike one as being a very resilient, close-knit family. I think there has never been very much feeling that this one is handicapped so he just gets treated as very normal which is probably the key to it all. He goes to an ordinary school and he's just treated as an ordinary child and I feel that's why there is no problem here.

Another caseworker talks in a similar vein about one of her families :

DS: This is a minimal handicap in that Diane wears a raised boot which her mother has always had a very accepting attitude towards. She's been able to cope with it very well herself and she's encouraged Diane in the idea that lots of people have got it; it's nothing to be ashamed of; it doesn't really stop you doing very much; you can keep up with all the others so get on with it. Now, Diane is getting more conscious of it as she is getting older, she's getting more worried about her appearance but Mum's got a very sensible attitude and the younger children really have no problems at all in this respect.

SK: So Diane's handicap hasn't really impinged on family relationship at all?

DS: No, not really because the mother's been able to cope and she's always treated Diane as a very ordinary kid, nothing special – just so far as she's been able.

On the whole it is not the degree of handicap as such which is important to the adjustment of siblings, but the degree to which the handicapped child is dependent on the parents. This is the crucial factor and the one most likely to bring about disruption in other relationships in the family.

In terms of the type of handicap suffered by a child, it has been shown by Goodman and others (1962) that both parents and children do have a rank order of preference for dealing with handicaps of various sorts. One might therefore expect certain sorts of disability to have a greater effect on a family than certain other sorts and there is, for example, some evidence to suggest that handicaps involving mental as well as physical impairment fall into this former category (Farber 1968). On the whole, however, it is the meaning of a handicap to parents that is most important, and this is not simply determined by the type or severity of the condition in question.

2. Age of sibling

If a child is sixteen or seventeen when a handicapped baby is born into his family, he is less likely to be affected in the same way or to the same extent as a much younger sibling. Margaret Adams drew attention to those problems of a specific nature which impinge crucially at difficult phases of the sibling's development. She distinguishes four stages as areas of specific stress.

i.	pre-school	–	up to five years of age
ii.	early school	–	from five to eight years of age
iii.	mid school	–	from eight to twelve years of age
iv.	adolescence	–	from twelve to eighteen years of age

Typical problems for each group are, according to Adams, i. not enough attention given to the sibling who responds with lowered demands (caseworkers reports would indicate the prevalence of the opposite reaction here : increased demands and attention seeking behaviour). ii. the sibling sees handicap from a new social angle, has guilty feelings on being healthy and feels worried that his own destructive 'sibling-rivalry fantasies' may have caused the condition. iii. social problems are made worse because of increased involvement. iv. fear about his own capacity for parenthood, ability to marry, etc. However accurate or otherwise these particular observations may be, the general principle that siblings face specific developmental problems in relation to handicap, is certainly good. Many sibling problems, therefore, will naturally be 'out-grown' as the sibling grows up.

3. Sex of sibling

It is well established (Sutton-Smith et al. 1964) that 'the sex of a given sibling has strong effects on adjustment, anxiety and interest inventories'.

When Stott's social adjustment guides are used, for example, there is a significant predominance of so-called 'disturbed' boys over girls. Perhaps this is because Stott's inventories are more sensitive to aggressive and anti-social behaviour. Macfarlane (1954), on the other hand, reports a far greater incidence of anxiety problems for girls than for boys. For the five-year-old age-group, he found 49 significant correlations between behaviour problems for girls but only 17 for boys.

We might conclude from this that the sex of a sibling might tend to have an effect on the way in which disturbance is experienced or expressed. There is no evidence as yet, however, to suggest that it makes the sibling either more or less susceptible to disturbance of some sort.

4. Size of family

Some caseworkers felt that siblings in large families stood a better chance of coping than siblings in small families. Other caseworkers felt the opposite. In fact there is no clear evidence to support either hypothesis. One can see, though, that children in large families are likely to find some recompense for parental neglect in their other brothers and sisters. On the other side of the coin, of course, they have more rivals for parental attention in the first place.

5. Birth order

Ann Gath found in her study of children with Down's Syndrome that 'there was a tendency for more deviant siblings to come from families where the handicapped child was not the youngest. Thus five deviant siblings came from three of the 10 families where the handicapped child was the first born or the middle born, whilst only two deviant siblings were from the 12 families in which the handicapped child was the last born'. These figures are not conclusive, however. For a start the sample is really too small to be meaningful. Furthermore, even if they are statistically viable, it could well be that the siblings from the families in which the handicapped child was the last born were assessed before the impact of the handicapped child had properly been felt, and therefore before their 'deviance' occurred. In the families assessed by caseworkers on my own questionnaire there was if anything a tendency for younger siblings to show disturbance more than siblings who were older than the handicapped child.

One factor which does seem to be significant in this respect is the relative ages of sibling and handicapped child respectively I have already looked in Chapter 5 at Farber's concept of the revision of birth-order roles in families whose life-cycle has been arrested. His results do seem to confirm the thesis that children closest in age to the handicapped child are more prone to disturbance in one form or another than children who are considerably older or younger than the handicapped child. He says that 'siblings who did not interact frequently with their retarded brother or sister generally were affected less than those who interact frequently'. And it has been established by Koch and others that siblings generally tend to interact more often with siblings who are near their own age than with those who are less close in age.

6. Religion as a force in the family

In some families religion was cited by caseworkers as being a positive force, though it must be said that many other families with strong religious beliefs were found to be in all sorts of difficulties.

One caseworker says of a Catholic family:

MR: The family seem to have copied mother; mother just grits her teeth and gets on with it and the children tend to copy this.

SK: Do you think the mother is worried underneath?

MR: I don't know, she just says 'what will be will be'. They are an Irish Roman Catholic family and they treat the whole thing in a very fatalistic way. They are very warm towards Michael and he gets a lot of attention and warmth at home.

This sort of comment raises the question of whether or not families with a religious belief are more easily able to accept the fact of handicap than those who have no such belief. An interesting study was conducted by Zuk (1970) into just this question. He looked at 79 parents of retarded children, 39 of whom were Catholic, 37 non-Catholic. The parents were interviewed in a non-sectarian hospital by an independent social worker. They were assessed as being 'acceptant' of their handicapped child if:

1. they showed minimal anxiety or hostility to the child when with him.

2. minimal defensiveness about the child's limitations.

3. neither obviously rejected the child nor fostered his overdependence on them.

After all the parents had been assessed in this way Zuk found a number of significant things :

1. Catholic mothers were more acceptant of their handicapped child than non-Catholic mothers.

2. All mothers were more acceptant of younger retarded children than older retarded children.

3. There was no significant relationship between the number of siblings and acceptance by either Catholics or non-Catholics.

Zuk suggests that the reason for the first of these findings is that the Catholic faith specifically absolves mothers from a sense of personal guilt for a severely handicapped and retarded child. As I have suggested there is not enough evidence yet to prove that siblings in religious families are less likely to be disturbed than siblings in other families. Indeed, as Zuk himself would seem to imply, religion as such is probably less important as a factor in determining the stability and wellbeing of families with a handicapped child than is parental acceptance of the realities of the situation and good parental adjustment.

7. Substitute parent figures

A number of siblings who were neglected by their parents seemed to find their own solution to this problem by adopting what could be regarded as a substitute parent figure. Strong attachments were developed with uncles, aunts and grannies with whom these children had previously had much more limited relationships. Many children also turned to their fathers for the fulfilment of needs which were previously met by the mothers. It has been demonstrated experimentally that for primates relations with contemporaries can to a large extent compensate for inadequate relations with parents (Harlow 1962), and many siblings who developed strong relationships with other siblings or with peers sometimes seemed to be fulfilling just this need in doing so.

8. Personality as a factor

Some children who have all the odds stacked against them somehow seem able to rise above their difficult situation and come
through not only unscathed, but if anything stronger and better
for their experience. When there is no apparent external factor
working for their redemption, such as the factors I have already
looked at, it is tempting to ascribe their ability to cope to their
own personality. There is of course a danger that we may use
personality as just a catch-all phrase to cover any factors that
cannot be located more precisely. But when all is said and done,
some children, like their parents do seem to have more internal
resources for coping with stress and adversity than others. One
such resource which undoubtedly has considerable importance
for the sibling of a handicapped child concerns his ability to
communicate his needs in an appropriate way. Lindy Burton
rightly says that

> '.... from infancy the child must be capable of expressing his
> tensions and attracting help from those around him. If he does
> not meet with immediate help he must be capable of modifying
> his methods of communication so that they become more
> appropriate for the expression of his desires. '

In terms of attracting attention it may well be that the more
extrovert outgoing child is at a distinct advantage, as in the
following family with able-bodied twins :

> 'It's difficult to say what Peter is feeling because he is a very
> quiet introspective child. He is doing well at school and things
> like this; he does have some friends, but he is an extremely
> difficult child to get to know because he is so introspective.
> He's somehow always in the background and he's certainly the
> neglected member of the family. Again here the two brothers
> are very different temperaments. William is the opposite; a
> very outgoing extrovert child, and as a result of this has
> always got a lot of attention from his parents. He has no
> trouble in finding friends. Somehow he's always able to contact
> his parents on the right level when he needs them, if you see
> what I mean.'

Another personal quality which appeared useful to siblings was
the ability to play down and de-fuse potentially disruptive situations. In the following family the nine-year-old handicapped

child was uncontrollably aggressive to everyone who came within reach. Once again the siblings here were twins.

DS: The mother says 'it's his way of communicating; how can I stop him?'

SK: Does he attack her as well?

DS: Oh yes, he comes for me too! He thumps anybody - he wants their attention.

SK: She doesn't mind this?

DS: No and he really thumps hard. He's a big boy. He's very obviously jealous of his mother paying attention to anyone other than himself. He gets very worked up when Mrs Mahoney is talking to me because he likes to monopolize all her attention.

SK: How do the other two children cope with this because there's only a two-year age difference. Do they protect themselves?

DS: They are twin boys and they cope amazingly well. Somehow they always manage to turn it into a game with the handicapped one. Obviously they have to protect themselves and fend him off but they deal with it just like a game and sort of turn it into a tumble on the floor. They're incredibly good-tempered and patient.

The personality of the sibling is important, then, particularly for the child who is old enough to realize that to a large extent he can be master of his own fate. The future of the sibling and the rest of his family is not pre-determined. With insight into the nature of their situation and courage to choose their own path they can mould a future of their own choosing, just as easily as the family that has never had any experience of handicap.

SENDING THE HANDICAPPED CHILD AWAY

I have already implied in a number of places that institutionalizing the handicapped child does not necessarily mean the end of emotional problems or, for that matter, practical ones for either parent or sibling.

   The conclusions of Caldwell and Guze, and of Professor Tizard after his careful study of this subject are quite clear. Tizard found that 12 per cent of families with a handicapped

child at home (150 families) had maladjusted or mentally backward children other than the defective one. For those families
with a defective child permanently placed in an institution (100
families altogether) 26 per cent had maladjusted or mentally
backward children other than the defective one. These results
clearly do not support the view that keeping a defective child in
the family upsets the other children more than when the defective child is institutionalized. On the other hand, and perhaps
this is contrary to appearances, neither do they support the
view that sending a defective child into an institution is more
likely to upset the other children in the family. What they do
suggest, according to Tizard, is that families with more than
one difficult child to cope with are likely to send the mentally
defective child to an institution.

Obviously if a child is sent away from the family the fears
and anxieties imposed on the remaining siblings are different
from those imposed on the sibling whose handicapped brother or
sister is at home. Some children may be better able to cope
with one sort of strain rather than the other, but there is no
available evidence to suggest that either situation is preferable
as a general rule.

CONCLUSION

In this chapter I have looked at a number of factors which are
likely to affect the able-bodied sibling's ability to cope, and one
or two factors which are not likely to affect it.

It is important to remember when talking about siblings of
the handicapped that they are not, as individuals, a strictly
homogeneous group. This means that any particular sibling
must always be regarded first and foremost as an ordinary,
individual child with his own unique life, his own unique problems
and his own unique solutions to those problems. At the same
time, however, one must remain aware of the possibility of
difficulties arising as a result of handicap. Parents, and caseworkers involved in such families, have a definite power which
may be used for better or worse to help the sibling over his
difficulties. These difficulties should not normally be regarded
as signs of a deep-seated pathology in the sibling, but rather as
an attempt by an essentially 'normal' child to come to terms
with a situation which is particularly difficult and stressful. The
same, of course, may be said of the parents and of the family as

a whole as it tries to adjust to the crisis of handicap. This
adjustment involves a social process which is common to all
'ordinary' families, and indeed to many other forms of social
organization insofar as they adjust to crises. For their adjustment represents an attempt to balance the internal and external
demands made upon them in such a way that the system as a
whole maintains a state of relative equilibrium.

As far as the sibling is concerned, it may not always be
easy to tell whether a child is coping satisfactorily or not.
Passive and quiet behaviour, as Underwood pointed out, is not
always a sign of contentment and happiness, nor is aggressive
behaviour necessarily a sign of maladjustment. Furthermore
there is some evidence that families with a handicapped child
are likely to put on a 'defensive front' concealing many of the
difficulties they encounter (Davis, p.115).

When difficulties are apparent, moreover, it may not
always be easy to tell whether or not they are related to handicap,
a point which one caseworker makes when she says of a client:

'Well, she bursts into tears very easily, but then again she's
a 15-year-old girl and she's very highly strung. If things are
going badly for her she'll easily fly into a temper and start
screaming and shouting. She's an adolescent and that way
inclined. It's not obvious to me why she's like that.'

One point, however, is clear, at least to most of the workers I
talked to, and that is that virtually all of the problems arising
for siblings as a result of handicap can effectively be overcome,
given the right home conditions and the right family attitudes.
Again a caseworker talks:

'It's interesting to see families where they are coping well.
As we're talking it seems to me – it's quite interesting from
my point of view, to note that the parents' attitude is so relevant. I mean you can have two families with the same type of
handicapped child and in one the siblings won't be affected
because the parents have got a certain attitude, whereas in
the other, say the mother's inability to cope or the father's
reluctance to help, can really put the sibling in jeopardy.

References

Adams, M. Siblings of the retarded, their problems and treatment. 'Child Welfare', XLVI, no. 6, 1967.

Begab, M. 'The Mentally Retarded Child - a Guide to Services of Social Agencies'. Children's Bureau publications, no. 404, 1963.

Burton, L. 'Vulnerable Children'. Routledge, London, 1968.

Buss, A. 'Psychopathology'. Wiley, London, 1966.

Caldwell, B. and Guze, S. A study of adjustment of parents and siblings of institutionalized and non-institutionalized retarded children. 'Amer. J. of Ment. Def. ', vol. 64, 1960, p 845.

Davis, F. 'Passage Through Crisis'. Bobbs-Merrill, USA, 1963.

Farber, B. 'Mental Retardation: its Social Context and Social Consequences'. Houghton and Mifflin, New York, 1968.

Gath, A. The mental health of siblings of congenitally abnormal children. 'J. Child Psychol. Psychiat.', vol. 13, 1972, pp 211-218.

Goodman, N. et al. Variant reactions to physical disabilities. 'Amer. J. of Ment. Def. ', vol. 66, 1962, pp 838-843.

Harlow, H. and Harlow, M. Social deprivation in monkeys. 'Scientific American', vol. 207, no. 5, November 1962.

Hewett, S. 'The Family and the Handicapped Child'. Allen and Unwin, London, 1970.

Koch, H. 'The relations of certain formal attributes of siblings to attitudes held towards each other and towards their parents'. Monograph 78, Society for Research into Child Development, 25 (4), 1960.

Macfarlane, J. W. , Allen, L. and Honzik, M. P. 'A Developmental Study of the Behaviour Problems of Normal Children between Twenty-one Months and Fourteen Years'. University of California publications in Child Development, vol. 2. University of California Press, Berkeley and Los Angeles, 1954.

Schreiber, M. and Feeley, M. Siblings of the retarded - a guided group experience. In 'Management of the Family of the Mentally Retarded'. Wolfensberger, W. and Kurtz, R.A. (Eds). Follett Educational Corporation, USA, 1969.

Sutton-Smith, B. and Rosenberg, B. G. Sibling association and role involvement. 'Merrill Palmer Quarterly', 10 (1) 1964, pp 25-28.

Sutton-Smith, B. and Rosenberg B. G. 'The Sibling'. HRW, USA, 1970.

Tizard, J. and Grad, J. C. 'The Mentally Handicapped and Their Families'. Oxford University Press, 1961.

Underwood, J. 'Report of the Committee on Maladjusted Children'. HMSO, London, 1955.

Zuk, G. Religious factors and the role of guilt in parental acceptance of the retarded child. In 'Counselling Parents of the Mentally Retarded'. Noland, R. (Ed.).Charles C. Thomas, Illinois, 1970.

12 Conclusion and proposals

My main thesis in this study has been roughly as follows: that it is neither adequate nor justifiable to view handicap, as has so often been done, simply as a tragedy for the individual child and a problem of care for the parents. Handicap is beyond doubt a disruptive event in the life of the family as a whole and it therefore has repercussions for the lives of each family member including able-bodied siblings. The effect on these siblings will to a large extent depend on the way in which the parents (and thus the family as a group) readjust after the practical and emotional upheaval that handicap brings.

I have chosen to focus on the siblings because, uninvolved in decisions relating to problems of care and rarely seen by professionals who come into contact with the handicapped, they have been virtually ignored both by researchers and by professional welfare agencies concerned with the problems of the disabled. Perhaps the reason for this is that only when we look at handicap purely as a family issue do the problems of siblings really begin to emerge.

All too often lip-service has been paid to a family perspective without the full implications of such a perspective being realized. The unease and ambivalence which underlies our society's attitude to handicap may well be responsible for the concentration of professional attention on the handicapped child himself and the consequent failure in really getting to grips with the social meaning of handicap both in the family and in the community.

I have drawn here from case-material and discussions on some 500 families in which there is a handicapped child, each family being visited currently by an ICAA worker. I have tried to identify and describe the main sources of stress for the able-bodied siblings in these families. Throughout this task it has been apparent that many different aspects of family functioning can be disrupted by the impact of a handicapped child. Amongst others, the following spheres of family life seem particularly prone to disruption: the parental distribution of affection and support amongst children in the family; the allocation of domestic responsibility; the allocation of blame for family disasters; the relationship between husband and wife. The exact reason for disruption in any of these spheres will vary from one family to another. Perhaps the handicapped child just physically demands a great deal of time and attention; perhaps the mother is moved by a sense of guilt to devote herself to him to the exclusion of the rest of the family. Whatever is the case, and there are many other possibilities, it is the sudden loss of equilibrium in the functioning of these areas of the family that is undoubtedly the major cause of sibling anxiety and disturbance. Far more so, for example, than the immediate physical presence of the handicapped child himself.

It follows from this that the emotional wellbeing of a sibling depends very largely on the way in which his family readjusts to the crisis of handicap. True, some of the sibling problems I have described are individual problems in the sense that they are not primarily a product of what is happening in the family as a group. A sibling's unjustified fear that he is a hereditary carrier of congenital disease, for example, or guilt that arises through the irrational fear that he is personally responsible for the disability of his brother or sister - such fears and fantasies spring directly from the confused emotions of the child and can be remedied only through careful work with the individual concerned. For the rest, however, the solution of the sibling's problems and the alleviation of unnecessary strain upon him is clearly contingent upon the restoration of an acceptable balance in the overall organization of family life.

If any single conclusion is to be drawn from this study, then, it is not that the siblings of the handicapped need attention in their own right, rather it is a reaffirmation of the old adage that 'a handicapped child is a handicapped family', and only when parents of the disabled, and the network of relevant social services that deal with them, can approach handicap from just this perspective will it be possible to alleviate on any meaningful scale the sibling disturbances I have described.

OBSTACLES TO THE RESTORATION OF FAMILY EQUILIBRIUM

How can the emotional stability of a family be restored following the various crises which handicap creates? What resources within the family itself and within the community at large can be mobilized to protect their integrity as a group? There seem to be at least four factors working against the restoration of a satisfactory equilibrium in families with a handicapped child and these must be properly understood by those wishing to help such families in a comprehensive and meaningful way.

1. The handicapped family faces certain special problems of care which actively disrupt the normal functioning of the family and often demand a readjustment of role relationships among its members. I have given an account of these specific care problems elsewhere – problems relating to the physical dependency of the child which demand a redistribution of time and attention on the part of the parents; behaviour difficulties arising from the handicap; special educational and medical needs; the difficulties of transportation and of finding suitable accommodation. The family as a social unit is required to absorb the full strain of meeting these immediate practical needs and it is often only by easing the burden of care in these various respects that one can ease the pressure which handicap exerts on the normal relationships within the family.

2. It is a characteristic of parents undergoing the sort of crises I have described to react to events on an instinctive level without being fully aware of what they are doing and without always realizing how their family as a whole is likely to be affected. Awareness and realization are by no means essential ingredients in the successful resolution of all family crises, but where it is a recurring feature of the crisis in question to divert attention from the everyday running of the family in the belief that the real problem lies elsewhere, then the importance of awareness is surely enhanced. Until the parents themselves begin to see handicap as a truly family event and not just in terms of the special needs of their handicapped child, then stability and equilibrium are bound to remain upset in some other, perhaps unnoticed, area of family life.

3. The third factor which may work against the restoration of equilibrium in family life is the fact that many parents are ignorant about the simplest facts of handicap and about where they can turn for help, guidance and support when these are wanted.

When a disabled child is discharged from hospital it is still commonplace rather than exceptional for the family to receive merely the statutory visit from a health visitor and thereafter to receive no other offer of specialized help. This is ironic in view of the vast array of different services and agencies which already exist in the hope of meeting the needs of these parents and their families. But until such formal support systems within the community can be seen by parents to be sharing realistically the responsibility for its handicapped citizens, then the brunt of that responsibility will continue to rest heavily on the already overburdened unit of the individual family, and casualties among its able-bodied members are bound to occur.

4. Finally in this respect, the family is further isolated within the community by the attitudes of the public at large. There is still a great deal of public embarrassment and ambivalence over the subject of handicap. I have already cited various instances of neighbours refusing to let their children play with retarded and handicapped children, misunderstanding the nature of handicap, and losing interest in visiting the handicapped family. There is no doubt that the social stigma which attaches to handicap is itself responsible for many of the problems faced by the handicapped and their families.

The physical limitations imposed by disability can often be overcome with minimal effort, but social discrimination is an enduring problem and the pervasive though often intangible stigma borne by the family as a whole eats away at parental confidence and plays upon feelings of guilt and shame.

Any realistic programme of help for families of the handicapped must, I believe, take into consideration all of these four factors which work against the successful resolution of family crisis. Many families will be able to help themselves out of their difficulty. For the rest, the external agents that exist within the community have an enormous part to play in helping families to regain their emotional balance after it has been upset by the arrival of a handicapped child. Assessment clinics, health visitors, parent groups, rehabilitation programmes and social work agencies have a therapeutic and preventive potential that has hardly begun to be realized as yet.

Although there are hundreds of agencies and organizations concerned with the disabled (Stone and Taylor), their respective functions are disparate and often highly specialized. The result is that income, education, rehabilitation, aids, institutionalization

and many other facets of disability may all be dealt with separately by these agencies without the effect of handicap on the
family as a whole ever being assessed. The 'secondary' problems
of handicap such as marital and sibling difficulties are therefore
more than likely to go unnoticed even when a professional is
involved in the case.

WHAT THEN CAN BE DONE?

Some form of systematic attempt to offer help and guidance to
families when they need it most must surely be instituted. At
present agencies such as ICAA come across numerous families
who are on the verge of a break-up or who have already broken
up and whose individual members are near desperation, all of
which could have been avoided if help had been available for them.
All of the evidence points to this need. Jessie Parfit talks
of:

'....the confusion and ignorance in which such parents are
often found; not knowing to whom to turn for accurate information, unaware of the facilities available to make life for their
children and themselves more bearable and further confused
by conflicting advice or half-truths. '

The Carnegie UK Trust which reported in 1964 after their study
of handicapped children and their families, laid down as one of
its major conclusions that:

'The importance of home background and maternal care has
not always been fully recognized. Emotional and practical
problems must be overcome before home care can be fully
effective. '

And Mandelbaum, who ran a group for parents of retarded children, reached the now familiar conclusion, that:

'Unless the parent can further resolve his hidden grief he
cannot fully release his capacity for profound understanding.
His previously unexpressed feelings of isolation, shock, frustration, anger, guilt, bitterness, must gradually be put into
words. His inner feelings of revulsion towards the handicapped
child, of harsh criticism, of fright and horror at the persistent
intrusion of death wishes, of loss of self-esteem, of defeat and
moments of victory must carefully be explored. '

· Conclusion and proposals

A conclusion which is endorsed by the words of a parent from
the United States (see Roberta Robinson, 1970):

> 'Our oldest boy (who is nine-years-old) is no more than an
> idiot. We accept that fact. But until that day four years ago
> when both of us faced it, we had no family life, we were on
> the brink of divorce, and Joyce teetered dangerously on the
> edge of insanity.'

Yet, however well documented the needs of such parents may be,
they are still not being met by the community at large. Indeed
the support systems which I have listed are simply not geared in
practise to cope with handicap on the level on which I have described it, that is as essentially a family event.

More co-ordination between the existing services is something
of a minimum requirement if this aim is ever to be achieved.
What is really needed is a thoroughly co-ordinated, systematic
service designed to meet the needs of the whole family, coupled
with a system of automatic referral by hospitals and doctors.
Such a service would be truly preventive in orientation and would
enable many families to readjust successfully to the problems
created by handicap before the adverse reactions described in
this book had the chance to occur.

A PREVENTIVE PROGRAMME

Since the 1963 Children and Young Persons Act one of the primary
concepts in social work with children has been that of prevention.
This has been most adequately defined by Kellmer Pringle (1965
p 133) as a range of services and activities designed to:

> 'help families through periods of temporary strain and crisis:
> to improve and, where necessary, supplement the quality of
> care and education of children considered "vulnerable" or to
> be "at risk" and to prevent the disintegration of the family unit.
> The keynote must be early and constructive intervention.'

Shortly after the Children and Young Persons Act was passed
a study was carried out by Aryeh Leissner prior to the setting
up of the family advice service. The report listed the following
objectives. (Leissner 1967 pp 18-19):
  a. the prevention of family breakdown;
  b. the prevention of children coming into care and/or
appearing before a juvenile court;

    c. the provision of an easily accessible source of help for all those in need of advice, guidance and assistance;

    d. the earliest possible detection of families and children at risk:

    e. the initiation and improvement of field-level co-ordination between the staff of relevant statutory and voluntary agencies;

    f. the provision of a community work service.

The same theme was taken up by the Seebohm report in the following year. This stressed 'the prevention of social distress' as the foremost task of an overall preventive approach. The report distinguishes between 'specific prevention', which it defines as action directed at helping families or individuals who are recognized to be at particular risk, whose problems are likely to generate further and more profound difficulties (para. 435), and 'general prevention', to be achieved 'by those universal services or policies which together reduce social and economic risk throughout the community' (para. 440).

By the turn of the last decade, then, prevention was widely accepted as one of the most important goals of social service agencies. Yet even today, some twelve years after the Children' Act was passed, hardly any truly preventive work is being done throughout the whole gamut of social work service. The statutory social services, for example, are rarely if ever involved in work with children other than those who are already showing signs of delinquency or distress. There are many reasons for this. One reason which is frequently put forward but rarely substantiated is that to tackle problems from the preventive end of the stick requires more resources than are at present available. A somewhat cynical rejoinder to this might be that preventive work requires an attitude on the part of the agency which is completely different from its current attitudes to intervention after things have gone wrong, and this change in thinking has simply not been forthcoming. Another reason for the conspicuous absence of real preventive work is the difficulty of identifying the children who are at risk before they show signs of serious disturbance.

In 1961 Gerald Caplan posed this problem:

'The major question is whether we have as yet any knowledge concerning noxious factors that are potent enough to change significantly the risk of mental disorder in a population of children amenable to alteration by preventive programmes.'

· Conclusion and proposals

There can be no doubt that today we do have a great deal of
knowledge about such factors, and handicap must surely be counted
among them. Moreover there can be few factors like handicap
which are so easy to identify in the population at large before they
have had any adverse effect on both the family and the child. The
birth of a handicapped child or the post-natal disablement of the
child must therefore be seen as ideal circumstances for the
implementation of a preventive programme. A glance back at
Kellmer Pringle's definition and Aryeh Leissner's list of objectives can only confirm the appropriateness of such a programme
in this context, a context which fulfils every requirement of
Seebohm's category of 'specific prevention'.

Obviously there are problems inherent in such a programme:
how, for example, would handicap be defined? Is the child whose
little finger is missing to be regarded as handicapped alongside
the child who is permanently brain-damaged and chair-bound? If
not where and how is the line to be drawn? How, in any event,
could automatic referral and appropriate intervention be made
in a way that would safeguard the privacy and freedom of the
individual family? To what extent would the casework side of
such a service concern itself with already existing problems
which have little immediate connection with handicap? How much
emphasis would be placed on support in crisis, guidance through
crisis, and the provision of advice and information respectively?
At what point would intervention cease? Who would be responsible for administering such a service? These questions and
many others would need to be answered, but there is no reason
to suppose that they could not be answered in an adequate way,
just as many of them were answered earlier in the century in
respect of the implementation of a preventive programme for
children in the field of medical health.

It would be wrong to imagine that a programme of preventive
social work in the field of handicap would eradicate distress or
conflict in the way that preventive medicine has effectively
eradicated poliomyelitis and rickets. What it could achieve,
however, is the widespread provision of help for families such
that all of their members can adjust in a constructive way to
potentially damaging experiences. It could develop strengths
within the family for coping with its special situation of stress.
And on a more practical level it could put these families in touch
with other families in a similar situation and with medical and
genetic counsellors. As a matter of course families would also

be informed of their welfare rights and the alternatives vis a vis the special educational and institutional options open to them.

The government is showing a growing recognition of the problems facing the disabled: in 1974 a parliamentary under secretary for state was appointed in the DHSS with, for the first time, special responsibility for the disabled. One can only hope that this new concern will not be tied to the old narrow-minded approach to disability, that is, seeing only the special needs of the disabled themselves, whilst ignoring, particularly in the early years of the child, the fact that disability is a family event. With the right approach and the right framework for the provision of help I believe there is good reason to suppose that the burden imposed by handicap on all family members, including the disabled themselves and their siblings, can be made considerably more bearable than it might otherwise be, and many of the specific difficulties facing respective members of the family can be forestalled.

The preventive measures that I have proposed are clearly not adequate on their own. They need to be effectively linked to a relevant programme of research and also to a greater awareness and sense of responsibility in the community at large.

In terms of research, a great deal more work needs to be done on the ways in which families react to handicap and on the possible associations between different sorts of family and different types of reaction. The researcher also has a wide-open field in terms of the sibling himself. Virtually no systematic research has been undertaken to determine the true proportion of siblings disturbed, nor for that matter the relative incidence of different sorts of disturbance amongst a sample of siblings. Such information is essential before any wide-scale programme of preventive work can be attempted. Quantitative methods of research could usefully pursue some of the following questions. Do siblings of the handicapped have significantly different attitude to childbirth from the attitudes of other siblings? Do they tend to have fewer children when they marry? Is the educational performance of these siblings significantly different from the educational performance of other siblings? Do the social attitudes of children with handicapped brothers and sisters differ markedly from those of children with able-bodied brothers and sisters? Do they, in fact, adopt more 'welfare norms'? Do male siblings of the handicapped display more aggression towards their peers outside the home than appropriately matched siblings

of able-bodied children? Do they tend to have more or less fears
and fantasies about hospitals? illness? death?

These and many questions like them are all amenable to
strictly controlled empirical analysis. Such analysis would be of
limited use to social workers and others working with individual
families and children, for the statistical treatment of such
questions can only show averages, general trends in a selected
population, and the family worker is never concerned with families
who are 'average'. What might be achieved, however, is a greater
awareness in government and the social services, at a policy
decision-making level, of a hitherto neglected aspect of the
meaning of disability.

In ancient Sparta, mentally retarded children were abandoned
to die of exposure. In late medieval times congenital deformity
was often seen as a mark of demonic possession. In the nine-
teenth and early twentieth centuries disability and deformity were
commonly associated with moral degeneracy and failure. Today
we flatter ourselves on having a more enlightened attitude to such
matters. No electoral manifesto is ever quite complete without
a promise or two for the disabled. Medical science is sponsored
and applauded for its efforts to keep children alive who in other
ages would certainly have died.

The welfare state is making slow but welcome progress in
recognizing the needs of this special minority group. But it is
ironic and inconsistent that whilst rightfully fighting for the lives
of handicapped children, accepting them as citizens with full
rights and professing concern over their special needs, the
powers that be seem content to see the social burden of handicap
rest solely on the individual family unit without offering them
help or information or advice. There is no standard procedure
of referral of these families to relevant welfare agencies,
parent organizations, etc.; no adequate education programme
for them; no help or support with their emotional, marital or
sibling problems, unless they seek it themselves from voluntary
sources. Furthermore in at least two London social work
colleges that I know of, the only initiation that students have into
the field of disability is to attend a solitary lecture on the
different sorts of medical disorder.

As I said to begin with, this sort of approach is neither
adequate nor justifiable, and until it is changed we cannot hope
to come to terms with the particular dimension of handicap
which I have explored in this book - that is as a social process

in which the family as a whole is engaged in crisis and readjustment, and the able-bodied sibling is at risk.

References

Caplan, G. (Ed.) 'Prevention of Mental Disorders in Children'. Tavistock Publications, 1961.

Carnegie UK Trust. 'Handicapped Children and their Families'. Dunfermline, Scotland, 1964.

Gould, B. Working with Handicapped Families. 'Case Conference', vol. 15, no. 5, 1968, pp 176-181.

Kellmer Pringle, M.L. The challenge of prevention. In 'Investment in Children'. Longmans, London, 1965.

Leissner, A. 'Family Advice Services: an exploratory study of a sample of such services organized by Children's Departments in England'. Longmans, London, 1967.

Leissner, A., Herdman, A. and Davies, E. 'Advice, Guidance and Assistance'. Longmans, London, 1971.

Mandelbaum, A. Groups for parents of retarded children. 'Children', vol. 14, no. 6, 1967, pp 227-232.

Parfit, J. 'Spotlight on Groupwork with Parents in Special Circumstances'. National Children's Bureau, 1971.

Richards, M. Role of the social worker in counselling and support. 'Developmental Medicine and Child Neurology', vol. 2, 1969, pp 786-791.

Robinson, R. In 'Counselling Parents of the Mentally Retarded', Noland, R.(Ed.). Charles C. Thomas, Illinois, 1970.

Stone, J. and Taylor, F. 'Handbook for Parents with a Handicapped Child'. A Home and School Council Publication, London, 1972.

Appendix A – The sample

1. SAMPLING PROCEDURE

The observations in this study were based on families being
visited by an ICAA caseworker. No special sampling procedure
was used except the omission of those families who did not fall
within the scope of the study. The following families were
omitted :

a. Families where there was no sibling over the age of
twelve months; children who were less than twelve months were
considered too young to be assessed.

b. Families who did not have more than one child based at
home. Children away at schools and boarding institutions were
considered to be based at home, even though they weren't
necessarily living there all the year round, whereas children
who had married or who had been fostered out were considered
to be part of a different family unit, and therefore based elsewhere. This interpretation of 'family unit' means that the
figures produced on family size pertain to the number of children
based at home at the time the interviews were carried out, which
does not necessarily correspond to the number actually produced
by the parents.

c. Families where there was no handicapped child. A small
number of cases had been taken on by the agency where a child
was presenting a behaviour problem but was not in any way
disabled.

d. Families where there was no able-bodied sibling.

e. Families where insufficient was known about the children
to make a reliable assessment. If sufficient was thought to be
known about even one sibling, the family was included in the
sample. This was largely left up to the discretion of caseworkers,
though in the follow-up interviews it became quite clear to what
extent each family was known by its caseworker. No families

were included if they had been visited by the caseworker in question for less than three months.

After these omissions had been made there remained 538 families being visited by 21 caseworkers in a total of 24 London Boroughs and parts of the counties of Kent and Surrey.

2. THE AGENCY AS A SAMPLING FRAME

Although nearly all the ICAA's caseload was used, these families are clearly not a random selection of families with a handicapped child. The agency itself constitutes a sampling frame and in assessing how representative these families are, account should be taken of the function of the agency, the way in which its referrals are sought and handled and the reasons why they are ultimately dropped or lost. All of these factors play their part in determining the sort of family to be found on the ICAA caseload at any given time and therefore contribute to any bias in the sample that was used.

a. Function of the agency

The main function of the ICAA is to provide support and casework help to any family which has or has had a handicapped child. The nature of help offered depends on the circumstances of the family and ranges from supportive visits on a very occasional basis to very intensive work with families where the handicap has caused crises of a major nature.

Although the service offered is primarily a casework service, some practical and financial help is also available for families in need and many families refer themselves in the first place for help of this sort. The agency helps families to claim the benefits for which they are entitled and is able to arrange, and sometimes finance, family holidays and outings for the children when these are not available from the local authority. Groupwork constitutes another important area of the agency's activity. A number of area offices run groups for handicapped adolescents and their siblings and also for the parents of the handicapped. Apart from enabling the respective family members to discuss and explore their problems, these groups put them in touch with other families who are in a similar position and who face similar sorts of problems.

One area office has a fully equipped and staffed playroom

designed to cater both for the handicapped child and his able-
bodied brothers and sisters.

The ICAA is involved in a number of other fields - it runs
five specialist residential schools, for example, but since the
families described in this book were drawn only from those using
the family casework service it is only necessary here to describe
this aspect of the agency's work.

b. Criteria for accepting referrals

The criteria for accepting referrals are fairly broad, providing
the family concerned :

    i.   lives in one of the areas covered by the agency;

    ii.   has a handicapped child under the age of eighteen.

There is no charge of any kind to clients for the services
offered, therefore the economic standing of clients is not inten-
tionally a relevant factor in the referral procedure. (See
Appendix D for figures on this.)

c. Source of referrals

The agency tries to encourage referral at an early stage after the
birth of the handicapped child but many referrals are made months
and even years after the birth itself which is indicative of the
abiding nature of many of the problems faced by such families.

Referrals come from the following sources and in roughly
the following order of frequency :

Hospital doctors and MSW's
Health visitors
Referrals by friends and relatives
Self referrals
Local authorities
GP's.

d. Geographical area from which families were drawn

All families in the sample lived in London or in the Home
Counties. Families came in varying proportions from the following London boroughs :

Barnet, Bexley, Brent, Bromley, Camden, Croydon,
Ealing, Enfield, Greenwich, Hackney, Hammersmith,
Haringey, Hounslow, Islington, Kensington and Chelsea,
Lambeth, Lewisham, Merton, Richmond, Sutton, Tower

Hamlets, Wandsworth, Westminster;   also from parts of Surrey and Kent.

e.   Nature of handicaps dealt with

Physical and mental disorders of every kind and severity are handled by the agency. Children, in the sample, were suffering from the following disorders :

Accident prone	1
Albright's disease	1
Amputation	3
Anterior horn cell disease	1
Arthrogryposis	7
Asthma	58
Ataxia	3
Athetosis	1
Autism	14
Battered baby	2
Behaviour problem	11
Bladder weakness	1
Bone marrow disease	1
Bowel weakness	3
Brain damage	23
Brain tumour	2
Brittle bones	4
Bronchiectasis	3
Bronchitis	7
Burns	3
Cerebral palsy	96
Chromosone deficiency	2
Coeliac disease	2
Compressed skull	2
Congenital dislocation of the hip	5
(Other) congenital deformity	17
(Multiple) congenital deformities	6
Convulsions	6
Cystic fibrosis	10
Deafness	19
Diabetes	8
Dwarfism	3
Dysplasia	1
Eczema	19

Emotional disturbance	13
Encopresis	2
Enuresis	6
Epilepsy	33
Epispadias	1
Gigantism	1
Haemophilia	3
Heart condition	27
Hirshopring's disease	2
Hydrocephalus	30
Hyperkinesia	4
Hypotonia	3
Icthyosis	1
Ileostomy	2
Incontinentia pigmenti	1
Leukemia	3
Malfunction of kidneys	7
Malnutrition	1
Medulloblastoma	1
Meningitis	2
Meningocele	1
Mental retardation	74 *
Metachromatic Leuko-dystrophy	1
Michrocephalus	5
Migraine	1
Mongolism	31
Muscular dystrophy	23
Muscular defect	7
Neurological condition	2
Obesity	1
Palate defect	7
Paralysis	29
Perthe's disease	1
Pituitary gland deficiency	1
Potter's syndrome	1
Reading difficulties	2
Rheumatic arthritis	1
Scleroderma	1

*This number includes only those cases where retardation was divorced from other diagnoses. For a full analysis of the occurrence of mental retardation in the sample, see Appendix D.

Sickle cell anaemia	3
Sight loss or defect	19
Speech loss or defect	16
Spina bifida	78
Spinal deformity	8
Still's disease	1
Talipes	3
Thalidomide	1
Toxemia	1
Tumour (other than brain)	1
Ulcer	1
Undescended testicle	1

The above table shows the number of times each disorder was diagnosed in the sample as a whole. As one would expect, there were a large number of families where more than one child had a disorder (there were 620 handicapped children altogether coming from 538 families). There was also a large number of children who had more than one disorder. The total number of entries in this table, therefore, does not tally with the totals in other tables.

When a child was suffering from more than one disorder each disorder was entered separately, thus one child might be entered more than once on the table. Hence there are 810 entries for a total of 620 children. The multiple entries were, in fact, often related (for example spina bifida and hydrocephalus or asthma and eczema), but many children had two or more conditions which appeared to be etiologically unrelated.

There are a number of difficulties in compiling a list of disorders such as this. For the sake of consistency I have tried to ignore the symptoms of a disorder and enter only under specific diagnostic categories. Thus, epileptic children were entered under 'epilepsy' but not under 'convulsions', which in this case would only constitute a symptom. This rule, however, was not always easy to apply, and one or two exceptions occurred where the diagnosis was still uncertain at the time of the enquiry; some entries were therefore made, for example, under 'convulsions' or 'bowel weakness', which might subsequently have been made under more precise diagnostic categories. Needless to say the diagnosis was in every case that of a doctor or specialist.

For certain disorders, the consequence was considered more significant than the initial disease. Cases of post-polio paralysis were therefore included under the general heading of 'paralysis' and rubella babies were listed under 'sight loss or defect' or 'deaf' as appropriate. Similarly, cases of brain damage resulting from meningitis and encephalitis were listed under 'brain damage'.

f. Caseworkers and their role in sampling

The agency, being voluntary rather than statutory, is able to accept only those cases which it wishes to accept. The caseworkers themselves decide whether or not a referral is appropriate and whether or not it can be accepted. On the whole they are not working under the same sort of pressure as their counterparts in social services departments and therefore they are not spending their time exclusively on 'crisis work', nor do they often turn cases down on the grounds of having too high a caseload. The agency generally is always looking for new referrals and in this sense the sample is not a selected one.

On the other hand the referring agents are often well established contacts who have come to know what is and what is not 'an ICAA case' and it is quite likely that on this account the sample is biased towards families presenting problems of a psycho-social sort rather than those who appear to have come to terms with the implications of handicap or those whose problems are chiefly practical or financial in nature.

It should also be remembered that families who have problems which are thought to be amenable to casework help are likely to be kept on the agency's register for considerable periods of time whereas other cases are likely to be closed much sooner.

Both of these factors would suggest that the agency's caseload at any given time is not strictly representative of all families with a handicapped child but is biased towards those families who have unresolved problems of the sort I have described.

Whilst one should clearly be aware of this bias, it may also be said that it does not unduly affect the contents of this report. My aim here has been not to make a statistical comparison between families with a handicapped child and those with able-bodied children, but quite simply to describe the problems faced by siblings of the handicapped. Although the suggested bias in the sample would affect our perspective on the overall size and extent of these problems, it would not affect our appreciation of the problems themselves. Indeed, all factors considered, the ICAA caseload is an ideal source of material for a study of the present kind; it contains families of every type, size and background who have children with an extremely wide range of disabilities of varying degrees of severity; these factors allow one considerable scope to explore all aspects of the problems facing their able-bodied siblings.

Appendix B – The questionnaire

The following instructions and questionnaire (one for each family visited) were sent to caseworkers prior to the detailed discussion of cases.

Note to caseworkers

In some families where there is a handicapped or retarded child the able-bodied brothers and sisters appear to be subjected to exceptional stresses and strains and, as a consequence, suffer from various forms of 'disturbance'. ICAA is making a study of the problems faced by these children, and your help and suggestions are very much required in this respect.

The purpose of the following questionnaire is to find out in roughly what percentage of ICAA's families there are 'disturbances' among the siblings, and to provide a basis for detailed case discussions at a later stage. Clearly the co-operation of everyone is necessary if we are to gain a clear overall picture of ICAA's caseload. You are asked therefore to fill out the questions and return the forms to Keith Grove, or to Central, as soon as you can. There will be no comparison between individual workers and in fact the name of the worker is not important here except for administrative reasons. Please be careful, however, not to duplicate information when, for example, one family is being seen by more than one worker. (In this case only one worker should count the family as his/her case.)

Each worker should receive two sets of forms : one containing sections A and B of the questionnaire, the other containing section C. The former of these has been filled out in ink to illustrate how this part of the questionnaire should be completed. It is concerned with demographic details of individual families

and a separate form should be used for every family you visit.
On the other form, containing section C, there is room to write
comments of a more general nature about your own experience
of the problems faced by siblings in the families you visit. You
may write about any aspect you consider important, and you are
welcome to write as much as you wish. Only one of these forms
need be filled out per worker.

If you have any doubts or queries about any part of the
questionnaire, please do not hesitate to ring me at Keith Grove,
and I will do my best to iron them out.

Stephen Kew
Keith Grove Centre

Notes accompanying section A of the questionnaire

Question 1. The purpose of this question is to establish some
basic facts about parents or their substitutes in
the home, i.e., is there a full complement (both
mother and father)? Are they the natural parents?
Has there been a death, divorce, or major separation? Refers only to the household. (Step-children
and adopted children should be counted as siblings,
though reference should be made to their status in
question 9.)

Question 4. The following criteria should be used when assessing the severity of a child's handicap.

	Slight	Marked	VS
Mental handicap	ESN	SSN	Vegetable
visible deform-ity i. e. what it looks like	In many situa-tions handicap might conceiv-ably go un-noticed even though in others it might be visibly obvious	would definitely be noticed at any time but still only a par-tial deformity in terms of total person	appears to affect total person. Whole person deformed

	Slight	Marked	VS
Mental handicap	ESN	SSN	Vegetable
Functional disability; degree of dependence measured according to developmental expectations	Could conceivably live or manage alone, but still likely to require help in certain specific tasks	not completely helpless but needs someone near for many tasks. Essentially unable to live alone	needs constant or very frequent attention and help in daily routine

Caseworker visiting:

SECTION A — THE FAMILY

1. Name ....
   (see accompanying notes)

                              Guardian....................

   Father .... Other ....

   Mother ....

2. Children by age on October 1st, 1971, birth order, and sex, ringing the handicapped child. Mark deceased children in correct birth order under age they would have been in October 1971. Include their date of death.

M						
F						
	1st	2nd	3rd	4th	5th	6th

3. Practical and financial circumstances:

   a. Poor. Low or irregular income. Would benefit from financial assistance, aid, holidays, re-housing.

   b. Adequate means. Just 'comfortable'. Able to cope. No serious housing problem.

   c. Affluent. Good housing and facilities. High standard of living.

4. Nature of disability of handicapped child. (Refer to children as 1st, 2nd, etc. as above if more than one is handicapped). See accompanying notes.

Medical diagnosis ....

....

Degree of :	None	Slight	Marked	V. Severe
Mental handicap				
Visible deformity				
Functional disability (need for aid in climbing stairs, eating, etc.)				

SECTION B — SIBLINGS

Care should be taken to refer to children throughout as 1st sibling, 2nd sibling etc. in exactly the same order as they are classified in Question 2.

5. Is there at present any evidence of emotional disturbance, behaviour disorder, or failure to adjust among any of the children (including the handicapped). Include all disturbances whether or not they appear to be related specifically to the impact of handicap. Signs of 'disturbance' might include anxiety symptoms, stammering, attention-seeking behaviour, delinquency, backwardness or withdrawal. Assessing 'disturbance' in such a simple way is not easy, but only a rough indication is required here. In each case the disturbance may be graded according to your assessment of its severity. (In any case of ESN, write 'ESN' in the appropriate grading.)

Insufficient known						
No disturbance						
Mild disturbance						
Seriously disturbed						
Child	1st	2nd	3rd	4th	5th	6th

6. For the children who are at present showing signs of disturbance show in which cases you consider the disturbance to have been precipitated by, or significantly exacerbated by some aspect of handicap or of its impact on the family.

Handicap has no effect						
Handicap partially responsible						
Handicap largely responsible						
Child at present disturbed	1st	2nd	3rd	4th	5th	6th

7. Show for which children (other than those already listed in question 5 and 6) there has been some evidence of disturbance in the past. Fill in the approximate age at which the problems appeared to cease.

Insufficient known						
Age at which problem ceased						
Child	1st	2nd	3rd	4th	5th	6th

8. For the children listed in question 7, show in which cases the disturbance appears to have been precipitated by, or significantly exacerbated by some aspect of handicap or of its impact on the family.

Handicap had no effect						
Handicap partially responsible						
Handicap largely responsible						
Child previously disturbed	1st	2nd	3rd	4th	5th	6th

9. Comments on Sections A and B.

SECTION C

There are no set questions to be answered in this Section; the space is intended for any personal comments you may have about the problems facing siblings, and you should regard the following as suggestions only. You may find that you cannot generalize about the problems you have encountered: that each was essentially different. This in itself would be useful to know. On the other hand, you may feel that certain recurrent problems of a practical or interpersonal nature seem to contribute more than others to siblings' difficulties. Comments about these and the parts played by age, sex and size of family would also be welcome, but it is important to write only from your own experience rather than guesswork, or simply because you feel you ought to comment on any particular item.

Please continue on additional sheets if necessary.

Thank you for your co-operation.

Appendix C – Caseworkers' comments on section C of the questionnaire

1. First of all, I must qualify what appear to be some of the effects of the handicapped child on the siblings by the fact that in the majority of my 'cases', the marriage relationship is unstable, if not very disturbed. One does not know to what extent the presence of the handicapped child has brought on the disturbance. In the more stable marital relationships the siblings do appear to have fewer problems. In some cases, the young sibling is very worried about the handicap and may be unable to leave the handicapped child in order to play with his 'normal' peers - this may be partly an identification with the mother's anxiety and guilt. On a practical level the siblings are often involved in the care of the handicapped child and may have to give up their free time in the holidays or after school in order to look after him/her. I have noticed a sibling's difficulty in expressing resentment about this and presumably the resentment is being expressed in other ways. The sibling may react to the disproportionate amount of attention his handicapped brother or sister is receiving by becoming ill or a problem himself.

2. In my caseload housing in all cases invariably makes the handicap worse than it might otherwise have been. In the case of spina bifida, for example, there is no room for them to exercise and often siblings are unduly restricted to allow the handicapped child more movement. For instance, toys not allowed out as they take too much space.

3. The pattern which emerges is not at all clear-cut. In the families on my caseload there are six who are mentally as well as physically handicapped. In five of these cases there is a slightly handicapped sibling and in one case there seems to be no obvious sign of disturbance in the siblings. The slight disturbance which I notice in some of the youngest siblings is in most

cases partly the result of their place in the family and the same might be said of eldest children who often feel rejected when number two comes along; this feeling gradually disappears when they settle at school. It is extremely difficult to generalize. Only one of my cases shows a definite disturbance in the second sibling which is felt to be the direct result of having a handicapped child.

4.   The large family seems to contain the handicapped child more easily than the small one. The problems experienced by siblings in these families tend to be related to sharing limited space and money rather than to missing out because of the needs of the handicapped. It seems probable that the only sibling of a handicapped child is in the most difficult position - parents require educational success at a high level to compensate for the lower level of achievement of the handicapped child and also expect help in entertaining or aiding the handicapped one. Mothers with two children are usually anxious to intellectualize about the problems of the normal child but some find it difficult to do much about it. Mental handicap slightly exacerbates this problem. In families where the marital situation is unsatisfactory, one feels that the handicapped child does not suffer but that the other children have to do more than they should. Equally, in such a situation it is not easy to weigh the different factors in the situation. In making each of these generalizations I can think of at least one family where what I am saying does not apply. So, though I do not feel that each family is essentially different, generalizations are only pointers to be considered with caution.

5.   A lot depends on the stability of the marriage and the intelligence and understanding of the mother. Where the youngest child is handicapped, particularly in a large family, siblings tend to continue to look upon him as a baby, and become 'natural' to him rather than becoming disturbed themselves. There is a good deal more jealousy of the attention given to a handicapped child, which is often of a transient nature and which could not be rated as 'disturbance'.

6.   To my surprise, I have found very little real disturbance due to the handicap of a sibling, and, where this has been present in any degree, this accentuated disturbance can be attributed to the parents' handling of the situation; this I feel points to the need of a worker helping parents with their feelings towards the handicapped child. It is also noted that parents who have had

good childhood experiences themselves can cope best with the handicapped child and his siblings - due, one finds, to their own ability to accept the handicap and not feel it is a reflection of their own inadequacies.

7.　If family communications improve, everything else seems to as well! In my caseload, marital problems and difficulties in family communication form a large part of the disturbances showing in the handicapped child and his siblings. (I think this is emphasized because I have a fairly high proportion of asthmatic children where psychosomatic elements generally play a large part - however, this can be seen in other families as well.) A handicapped child can add to an already difficult situation in the family's relationships with one another. Bad communication can break down even more with a handicapped child because of mutual recrimination between husband and wife and their guilt feelings, thus causing more disturbance. A handicap (particularly a very bad one) can also sometimes cause disturbance in siblings from happier families - mainly because of lack of parental attention because they are too tired and busy looking after the handicapped child. Sometimes the handicapped child can find it more difficult than ever coming to terms with his own handicap if he is over-protected by his parents. Given a family where communication is reasonably good or can be improved, the siblings generally seem able to learn gradually to get their share of attention in an acceptable way. There are some families where the parents are particularly caring and responsible, and can shield the handicapped child and siblings from disturbance; but they often need an outlet for the tension building up in themselves.

Appendix D – Statistics

The statistics presented in this appendix relate sibling disturbance (as assessed by caseworkers) to a number of other factors. Table 1 relates it to family size; table 2 to the financial means of the family; and the three parts of table 3 to the degree of severity of handicap.

When trying to interpret these statistics we should clearly bear in mind that the assessments were in all cases subjectively made, although an attempt was made at a briefing session to standardize the way in which caseworkers would assess any given child. These assessments were intended primarily to act as a starting point for more detailed case-discussions, and not in the first place to yield statistical data of the sort presented here.

What this means, basically, is that the information they convey about the families themselves is compounded with information about the way in which the caseworkers concerned saw those families. Needless to say, these are two different things, and ideally we would want to see them presented separately. However, they are not without interest as they stand, and they are therefore included in this appendix in the hope that at very least they will prompt some more viable attempt at assessment in the near future.

Table 1 shows that there is very little difference between families of different sizes in terms of the likelihood of caseworkers rating one or more of the siblings either mildly or seriously disturbed. However, if we break down the disturbance into separate categories of mild and serious, we see a different pattern emerge. Smaller families emerge as being quite clearly more likely to contain a child rated mildly disturbed (40. 7 per cent of two-child families come into this category; 42. 2 per cent of three-child families) than large families (only 28. 8 per cent of five-child families come into this category and 25.6 per cent of six-child families).

If we look at children rated seriously disturbed, however, this trend is completely reversed. Small families are less likely to have a child rated seriously disturbed (6.6 per cent of two-child families and 7.0 per cent of three-child families come into this category) than large families (19.2 per cent of five-child families come into this category and 15.3 per cent of six-child families).

We cannot be certain what these results mean. However there are two possible sorts of interpretation:

1. that the smaller the family the more prone the siblings are to be mildly disturbed but the more likely they are to have serious disturbance forestalled; whilst in larger families siblings are less likely to suffer from minor disturbances, but when they are badly disturbed this is less well coped with and contained.

Or alternatively:

2. that caseworkers are more likely to view disturbed siblings in small families as being mildly disturbed, but disturbed siblings in large families as being seriously disturbed.

Clearly there is a difference between these two interpretations, but whichever one proves correct there will be some interesting and important implications.

The data contained in table two relates sibling disturbance to the financial means of the family. Families were divided into three categories, A, B and C (see questionnaire for the criteria pertaining to each category). The results show little difference between these different sorts of families in terms of the likelihood of siblings being rated disturbed. C families are less likely to contain siblings rated seriously disturbed than are the other sorts of family, but this is the only significant figure.

Table 3 relates sibling disturbance to the degree of severity of handicap. This was assessed using three different dimensions of handicap: mental handicap, visible deformity and functional disability (see note attached to the questionnaire for the criteria pertaining to each of these). The results in this section show that for each dimension of handicap the likelihood of a sibling being rated disturbed increases with the degree of severity of handicap. However when we distinguish between mild and serious disturbance there is no clear pattern, except in those families where there was no handicap in the particular dimensions looked at, and in these the siblings were consistently rated as having fewer mild disturbances than siblings in the other families.

TABLE 1 : SIBLING DISTURBANCE RELATED TO SIZE OF FAMILY

N.B.   Only those 'disturbances' felt by caseworkers to be caused (either partially or wholly) by handicap are included in this table.

Size of family	Total No. of families of each size	Families containing at least one sibling rated mildly disturbed (but not seriously disturbed) :		Families containing at least one sibling rated seriously disturbed :		All families containing a sibling rated disturbed (either mildly or seriously) :	
		Total No. of families	Percentage of each size group	Total No. of families	Percentage of each size group	Total No. of families	Overall percentage of each size group
2 children	182	74	40.7%	12	6.6%	86	47.3%
3 children	142	60	42.2%	10	7.0%	70	49.2%
4 children	113	34	30.1%	9	7.8%	43	37.9%
5 children	52	15	28.8%	10	19.2%	25	48.0%
6 children	39	10	25.6%	6	15.3%	16	40.9%
7 children	7	2	28.5%	2	28.5%	4	57.0%
8 or more children	3	1				1	

TABLE 2 : SIBLING DISTURBANCE RELATED TO FINANCIAL MEANS OF FAMILY

N.B. Only those 'disturbances' felt by caseworkers to be caused (either partially or wholly) by handicap are included in this table.

Classification of family*	Total No. of families for each classification	Families containing at least one sibling rated mildly disturbed (but not seriously disturbed) :		Families containing at least one sibling rated seriously disturbed :		All families containing a sibling rated disturbed (either mildly or seriously) :	
		Total No. of families	Percentage of total class group	Total No. of families	Percentage of total class group	Total No. of families	Overall percentage of class group
A families	171	55	36.7%	17	9.9%	72	42.1%
B families	309	117	37.8%	29	9.3%	146	47.2%
C families	58	22	37.9%	1	1.7%	23	39.7%

* See question 3 on the questionnaire

TABLE 3 : SIBLING DISTURBANCE RELATED TO SEVERITY OF HANDICAP

A. DEGREE OF MENTAL HANDICAP

Degree of mental handicap (see note accompanying questionnaire)	Total No. of families with children in each class *	Families containing at least one sibling rated mildly disturbed (but not seriously disturbed) :		Families containing at least one sibling rated seriously disturbed :		All familes containing a sibling rated disturbed (either mildly or seriously) :	
		Total No. of families	Percentage of total class group	Total No. of families	Percentage of total class group	Total No. of families	Overall percentage of class group
None	251	70	27.8%	21	8.3%	91	36.2%
Slight	115	48	41.7%	10	8.7%	58	50.4%
Marked	94	39	41.7%	7	7.4%	46	48.9%
Very Severe	80	38	47.5%	12	15.0%	50	62.5%

*Where there was more than one handicapped child in a family, the most severely handicapped was the one assessed for the purpose of this table. The same applies to parts B and C of this table.

189

TABLE 3: SIBLING DISTURBANCE RELATED TO SEVERITY OF HANDICAP (Continued)

B. DEGREE OF VISIBLE DEFORMITY

Degree of visible deformity (see note accompanying questionnaire)	Total No. of families with children in each class	Families containing at least one sibling rated mildly disturbed (but not seriously disturbed):		Families containing at least one sibling rated seriously disturbed:		All families containing a sibling rated disturbed (either seriously or mildly):	
		Total No. of families	Percentage of total class group	Total No. of families	Percentage of total class group	Total No. of families	Overall percentage of class group
None	163	41	21.4%	13	7.9%	54	33.1%
Slight	157	65	41.4%	14	8.9%	79	50.3%
Marked	170	69	40.6%	15	8.8%	84	49.4%
Very Severe	50	21	42.0%	7	14.0%	28	56.0%

TABLE 3 : SIBLING DISTURBANCE RELATED TO SEVERITY OF HANDICAP (Continued)

C. DEGREE OF FUNCTIONAL DISABILITY

Degree of functional disability (see note accompanying question-naire	Total No. of families with children in each class	Families containing at least one sibling rated mildly disturbed (but not seriously disturbed) :		Families containing at least one sibling rated seriously disturbed :		All families containing a sibling rated disturbed (either seriously or mildly) :	
		Total No. of families	Percentage of total class group	Total No. of families	Percentage of total class group	Total No. of families	Overall per-centage of class group
None	161	35	21.7%	15	9.0%	50	31.6%
Slight	132	52	39.3%	11	8.3%	63	47.7%
Marked	137	53	38.7%	12	8.7%	65	47.4%
Very Severe	110	55	50.0%	11	10.0%	66	60.0%

Index

Index

Index